the NELSON FIRST CERTIFICATE *course*

Teacher's Book

Susan Morris, Alan Stanton

Addison Wesley Longman Limited
Edinburgh Gate
Harlow
Essex
CM20 2JE
England
and Associated Companies throughout the world.

First published by Thomas Nelson and Sons Ltd 1993
This edition Longman Group Ltd 1996

Set in Helvetica, Futura, New Century Schoolbook

Printed in Spain
by Gráficas Estella

Second impression 1996
ISBN 0 17 557130 9

Acknowledgements
We are grateful to the University of Cambridge Local Examinations Syndicate for permission to use the specifications for the revised FCE examination on pages 6 to 11.

Contents

INTRODUCTION

The Nelson First Certificate Course provides students with comprehensive preparation for the First Certificate in English examination. The course consists of a Students' Book, two class cassettes, an Exam Practice cassette, a Workbook and a Teacher's Book containing answers, tapescripts and advice on using the course.

Organisation of the Students' Book

There are twenty ten-page units in the Students' Book, each based around a theme.

Lead-in

Each unit begins with a lead-in, which is designed to start students thinking and talking about the theme of the unit. The first part of the lead-in consists of a photograph or other iiiustration and exercises to stimulate discussion of the theme. The second section contains a variety of vocabulary exercises which cover the core vocabulary needed to talk and write about the theme of the unit. Many of the words that occur in the reading passages can be found in these lead-in exercises, so providing an opportunity for the pre-teaching of vocabulary.

Reading

There are three reading texts in each unit, the first coming after the lead-in section. All three can be studied in class, but teachers may wish to set one reading text as an individual homework assignment. Reading texts have pre-reading questions, which are designed to relate aspects of students' life to the theme of the text, exercises on vocabulary and comprehension questions of various kinds. The texts are chosen from a variety of contemporary sources.

Grammar

Each unit deals with a major grammar topic. At the end of the book there are Grammar Notes. These are not intended to provide a comprehensive description of English grammar. The Grammar Notes are directly related to particular exercises in each unit. Students may use the notes before, during or after doing the grammar activities, as the teacher decides. The Grammar Notes are also linked to some of the exercises in the English in Use section.

Listening

Each unit has two listening sections. There is a mixture of authentic, semi-scripted and scripted material and a wide range of question formats. There is a large number of different speakers, various accents and a mixture of monologues, dialogues and group discussions. Each listening text should be played to the students at least twice but, in general, the authentic passages need to be played at least three times. It is useful for students to answer the questions working alone but in some cases discussion is required.

English in Use

This section will be found on the fifth and tenth page of each unit and helps prepare students for Paper 3 of the First Certificate examination. It includes vocabulary items, word-formation exercises, phrasal verbs and grammar points. Guidance is given in how to find errors and a number of exam style questions are included. Gapped texts are also used frequently to familiarise students with a format found in the First Certificate examination. In exercises of this type students should first read through the text carefully to gain a clear idea of the subject of the text before attempting to fill the gaps. Grammar Notes are also linked to some of the exercises in this section.

Talking Points

The Nelson First Certificate Course provides many opportunities for speaking throughout every unit both in the Lead-in section and in the pair and group work exercises which are linked to the Reading and Listening texts, and the Grammar section. There is also a specific section of each unit which is devoted to speaking skills, called Talking Points.

Talking Points occurs towards the end of each unit, to allow the students the opportunity to make use of new vocabulary and phrases that have appeared in the unit up to this time. Fluency in speaking is an important aspect of student performance in Paper 5 of the First Certificate examination and students should be encouraged to develop their confidence, particularly in areas that are familiar everyday topics. Teachers should monitor students carefully while they work on this section so that any errors in vocabulary or grammar can be picked up and dealt with immediately after the Talking Points activities.

The themes of Talking Points stem from the content of the unit as a whole and represent a slightly different aspect from the areas already covered. Students should therefore have no difficulties with the core vocabulary, but again monitoring will show if the teacher needs to prompt or to provide further practice in specific areas. Stimuli for the Talking Points section range from photographs to poems and there are a variety of tasks of the type included in Paper 5 of the First Certificate examination.

Writing

The Writing section covers Paper 2 of the First Certificate examination. There is practice in a range of writing skills including letter writing, narrative, summary and discursive writing. In every case, there is something for the student to read and respond to in writing, as well as examples and advice on how to proceed.

Exam Practice

There are four sets of Exam Practice pages. These consist of specific examination practice for Papers 1, 3 and 4. All the different formats for Paper 1 (Reading), Paper 3 (Use of English) and Paper 4 (Listening) are covered in these pages. They provide useful preparation and practice for the exam since they mirror the format of the new First Certificate examination. Additional exam hints are included at the back of the Students' Book and give guidance in how to approach the different exam questions.

Organisation of the FCE examination

Paper 1 – **Reading**

Paper Format

The paper contains 4 parts. Each part contains a text and corresponding comprehension tasks. One part may contain 2 or more shorter related texts.

Length of texts

1900 – 2300 words approximately overall; 350 – 700 words approximately per text.

Number of Questions

35.

Text Types

From the following: advertisements, correspondence, fiction, informational material (e.g. brochures, guides, manuals, etc.), messages, newspaper and magazine articles, reports.

Task Types

Gapped text, multiple choice, multiple matching.

Task Focus

Understanding gist, main points, detail, text structure or specific information, or deducing meaning.

Answering

For all parts of this paper, candidates indicate their answers by shading the correct lozenges on an answer sheet.

Timing

1 hour 15 minutes.

Part	Task Type and Focus	Number of Questions	Task Format
1	Multiple matching Focus as for whole paper	6 or 7	A text preceded by multiple matching questions. Candidates must match a prompt from one list to a prompt in another list, or match prompts to elements in the text.
2	Multiple choice Focus as for whole paper	7 or 8	A text followed by 4-option multiple choice questions.
3	Gapped text Understanding gist, main points, detail and text structure	6 or 7	A text from which paragraphs or sentences have been removed and placed in jumbled order after the text. Candidates must decide from where in the text the paragraphs or sentences have been removed.
4	Multiple matching, Multiple choice Focus as for whole paper	13 –15	As Part 1.

Paper 2 – **Writing**

Paper Format

The paper contains 2 parts.

Number of Tasks

Candidates are required to carry out two tasks; a compulsory one in Part 1 and one from a choice of four in Part 2.

Task Types

From the following: letters, articles, reports, compositions, written for a given purpose and target reader.

Answering

The overall word length of answers across the two tasks is 240 – 360 words

Timing

1 hour 30 minutes.

Part	Task Type and Focus	Number of Tasks and Lengths	Task Format
1	**Q 1** Writing a transactional letter.	1 compulsory task 120–180 words	A situationally-based writing task giving candidates guidance to the situation through 1–3 short texts and sometimes visual prompts, as well as rubric.
2	**Q 2–4** Writing one of the following: • an article • a non-transactional letter • a discursive composition • a descriptive/narrative composition/short story • a report	4 tasks from which candidates choose 1 120–180 words	A situationally-based writing task presented through rubric or a composition topic presented through rubric.
	Q 5 Writing one of the above on a prescribed background reading text.	Q 5 there are 2 options	A task presented through rubric.

Paper 3 – **Use of English**

Paper Format

The paper contains 5 parts.

Number of Questions

65.

Task Types

Multiple choice cloze, open cloze, 'key' word transformations, error correction, word formation.

Answering

For all parts of this paper candidates write their answers on an answer sheet.

Timing

1 hour 15 minutes.

Part	Task Type and Focus	Number of Questions	Task Format
1	Multiple choice cloze An emphasis on vocabulary	15	A modified cloze text containing 15 gaps and followed by 15 four-option multiple choice questions.
2	Open cloze Grammar and vocabulary	15	A modified cloze text containing 15 gaps.
3	'Key' word transformations Grammar and vocabulary	10	Discrete items with a lead-in sentence and a gapped response to complete using a given word.
4	Error correction An emphasis on grammar	15	A text containing errors. Some lines of the text are correct, other lines contain an extra and unnecessary word which must be identified.
5	Word formation Vocabulary	10	A text containing 10 gaps. Each gap corresponds to a word. The 'stems' of the missing words are given beside the text and must be transformed to provide the missing word.

Paper 4 – **Listening**

Paper Format

The paper contains 4 parts. Each part contains a recorded text or texts and corresponding comprehension tasks.

Number of Questions

30.

Text Types

From the following:

Monologues: answerphone/freephone messages, commentaries, documentaries/features, instructions, lectures, news, public announcements, publicity/advertisements, reports, speeches, stories/anecdotes, talks.

Interacting speakers: chats, conversations, discussions, interviews, quizzes, radio plays, transactions.

Recording Information

Each text is heard twice.

Recordings will contain a variety of accents corresponding to standard variants of English native speaker accent, and to English non-native speaker accents that approximate to the norms of native speaker accents.

Background sounds may be included before speaking begins, to provide contextual information.

Task Types

From the following: multiple choice, note taking, blank filling, multiple matching, selection from 2 or 3 possible answers.

Task Focus

Understanding gist, main points, detail or specific information, or deducing meaning.

Answering

Candidates indicate their answers by shading the correct lozenges or writing the required word or words on an answer sheet.

Timing

Approximately 40 minutes.

Paper 4 – **Listening**

Part	Task Type and Focus	Number of Questions	Task Format
1	Multiple choice Understanding gist, main points, function, location, roles and relationships, mood, attitude, intention, feeling or opinion.	8	A series of short unrelated extracts, of approximately 30 seconds each, from monologues or exchanges between interacting speakers. The multiple choice questions have three options.
2	Note taking or blank filling Understanding gist, main points, detail or specific information, or deducing meaning.	10	A monologue or text involving interacting speakers and lasting approximately 3 minutes.
3	Multiple matching As for Part 1.	5	A series of short related extracts of approximately 30 seconds each from monologues or exchanges between interacting speakers. The multiple matching questions require selection of the correct prompt from a list of prompts.
4	Selection from 2 or 3 possible answers As for Part 2.	7	A monologue or text involving interacting speakers and lasting approximately 3 minutes. The questions will require candidates to select between 2 or 3 possible answers, e.g. true/false; yes/no; three-option multiple choice; which speaker said what, etc.

Paper 5 – **Speaking**

Paper Format

The paper contains 4 parts.

The standard format is two candidates and two examiners.

One examiner acts as both assessor and interlocutor and manages the interaction either by asking questions or providing cues for the candidates. The other acts as assessor and does not join in the conversation. *(Note that the individual test format may be used in certain examination centres.)*

Task Types

Short exchanges with the examiner and with the other candidate; a 'long turn' of about one minute.

Task Focus

Exchanging personal and factual information, expressing and finding out about attitudes and opinions.

Timing

Approximately 15 minutes.

Part	Task Type and Focus	Length of Parts	Task Format
1	Short exchanges between each candidate and the interlocutor. Giving personal information/ socialising.	4 minutes	The interlocutor encourages the candidates to give information about themselves.
2	Long turn from each candidate, with a brief response from the other candidate. Exchanging personal and factual information, expressing attitudes and opinions; employing discourse functions related to managing a long turn.	4 minutes	The candidates are in turn given visual prompts (two colour photographs) which they talk about for approximately a minute. They are also asked to comment briefly on each other's photographs.
3	Candidates talk with one another. Exchanging information, expressing attitudes and opinions.	3 minutes	The candidates are given visual prompts (photographs, line drawings, diagrams, etc.) which generate a discussion through engaging in tasks such as planning, problem solving, decision making, prioritising, speculating, etc.
4	Candidates talk with one another and the interlocutor. Exchanging and justifying opinions.	4 minutes	The interlocutor encourages discussion of matters related to the theme of Part 3.

unit 1 PEOPLE AND CLOTHES

This unit is intended to reactivate and develop vocabulary used for clothing and physical appearance. Teachers should encourage students to develop their fluency and accuracy as well as to master some of the more challenging vocabulary which is presented in the unit.

Lead-in (page 6)

1 The aim of these photographs is to prompt students to use the vocabulary of description of people, including characteristics such as height, build and colouring as well as what people are wearing. Some vocabulary has been supplied in the Students' Book to provide a starting point. Students should work together in small groups, describing the photographs and discussing the questions.

The photograph top left shows a young woman with dark hair wearing a smart red suit and carrying a briefcase. The photograph immediately below shows a young man, probably a telephone engineer, wearing blue overalls and a yellow helmet. The photograph top right shows a young nurse with blond hair and a fringe. She is wearing a purple nurse's uniform and is holding a baby in her arms. The photograph bottom right shows a young man, an American footballer, with dark hair who is wearing a helmet with a visor and a lot of padded clothing.

2 The labelling exercise provides an opportunity to practise vocabulary items for parts of the body which may be less familiar to the students. Again students should work in pairs or small groups.

1	h	8	i
2	n	9	k
3	l	10	c
4	a	11	f
5	e	12	d
6	g	13	m
7	j	14	b

3 Check first that the students know the words that appear in the box and explain any that are not familiar to them. Students can work alone or in pairs on the task of filling the gaps, before checking the answers with the whole class. The activity could also be done as homework in preparation for the next class.

1	pimples	5	face-lift
2	bags	6	cream
3	greasy	7	wig
4	frayed	8	patched

Reading: *Who are these people?* (page 8)

1 The reading text and the task can be done in pairs or groups.

1 fitness expert/keep-fit instructor/aerobics instructor
2 walker/climber
3 down and out/tramp
4 schoolboy
5 customs official/immigration officer/policewoman

2 He is short and slightly overweight. He looks middle-aged and is bald. He has got a beard and moustache and heavy eyebrows. His nose is long and straight.

She is of average height, is slim and looks in her late thirties. She's got short dark curly hair with a parting on the left side. She has a tanned complexion.

She is tall and young – about sixteen. She's got shoulder-length straight blond hair with a heavy fringe. She's got a fair complexion with freckles.

Grammar: *present simple, present continuous* (Grammar Notes **1.1** and **1.2**) (page 9)

1 Students should work in pairs on these exercises in class.

1	meet	5	am meeting/seeing
2	see	6	melt
3	wears	7	make
4	is making	8	is paying

9	does not melt	14	are melting
10	is wearing	15	makes
11	am meeting/seeing	16	is making
12	am not making	17	melts
13	pays		

2

1a	are you staying	6a	Does he look
1b	Do you stay	6b	Are you looking
2a	Do you eat	7a	are you putting
2b	Are we eating	7b	do I put
3a	Do you cook	8a	don't you go
3b	are you cooking	8b	are you going
4a	do you think	9a	Does he sleep
4b	are you thinking	9b	Is … sleeping
5a	Are you walking		
5b	Do you walk		

Listening: *In a shop*

(Grammar Notes **1.3**) (page 10)

Tapescript

1 CUSTOMER: What size are they?
SHOP ASSISTANT: Size 36, madam.
CUSTOMER: No, I don't think it's worth trying them on. Haven't you got size 38?
SHOP ASSISTANT: I'm afraid not, madam.

2 CUSTOMER: Can I have a look at that handbag, please?
SHOP ASSISTANT: Certainly madam. It's genuine leather. Made in Italy.
CUSTOMER: How much does it cost?
SHOP ASSISTANT: £249, madam.
CUSTOMER: I'm afraid that is a little out of my price range.

3 CUSTOMER: These trousers don't fit very well around the waist. Have you got the next size up?

4 CUSTOMER: I know this T-shirt is supposed to be baggy but I really think I need a small rather than a medium.

5 CUSTOMER: Have you got this pullover in another colour?
SHOP ASSISTANT: Not in the same size, sir.
CUSTOMER: That's a pity. I like the style but this colour – it hurts my eyes just looking at it.

6 CUSTOMER: It's very good quality, I can see that, but I couldn't wear this material next to my skin. It would make me itch.

7 SHOP ASSISTANT: This coat is in your size, madam.
CUSTOMER: But I don't think I want to try it on. Even my mother wouldn't wear a coat in that style.

8 CUSTOMER: It looks very smart but it gets very cold on the ski slopes and I need a jacket with a lot more padding.

9 CUSTOMER: It's a nice dress and it would be all right for a party but not for an interview.

10 SHOP ASSISTANT: I'm afraid we're out of stock at the moment, sir, but we have more coming in on Friday, if you would like to place a special order.
CUSTOMER: I'm afraid that's no good. I'm going on holiday tomorrow.

A

1	too small	6	too rough/itchy
2	too expensive	7	too old-fashioned
3	too tight	8	too thin/ light
4	too big/loose	9	too informal/casual
5	too bright	10	too late

Tapescript

JANE: Excuse me, my sister gave me this pullover as a birthday present but unfortunately it's the wrong size. It's too small.
SHOP ASSISTANT: I see. Have you got the receipt, madam?
JANE: Well, no, because she posted it to me from Portsmouth where she lives and she didn't enclose the receipt.
SHOP ASSISTANT: So, she didn't buy it here?
JANE: No, from your branch in Portsmouth, but it's obviously one of yours – your name is on the label.
SHOP ASSISTANT: Yes, of course.

JANE: It's not a problem, is it? After all, I think my sister bought it from a shop with branches nationwide just in case I wanted to change it.

SHOP ASSISTANT: Well, would you like to choose a pullover in your size?

JANE: Well, the problem is, I've already looked and actually I couldn't find one in my size in this colour – and it's the only colour I like. So I think that, actually, I would like to have a refund.

SHOP ASSISTANT: Certainly, madam, but you will have to take the pullover to the refund cashier on the second floor.

JANE: Right. Thank you.

B
1 A pullover.
2 It was the wrong size/It didn't fit.
3 Her sister.
4 It was too small.
5 The receipt.
6 No.
7 A chain store.
8 No, because they didn't have her size in the colour she wanted.
9 She got a refund/ She got her money back.

English in Use: *Comparative, superlative* (Grammar Notes **1.4**) (page 10)

1
1 John and Edward are the same height.
2 The suitcase and the bag are the same weight/both weigh the same.
3 The diamond ring and the emerald ring are the same price/both cost the same.
4 The kitchen and the bathroom are the same size/both measure the same.
5 The shelves are the same width.
6 The Tropic of Cancer and the Tropic of Capricorn are the same distance from the Equator.
7 Today the temperature is the same in Tokyo and London.
8 My motorbike and my car can reach the same speed/are as fast as each other.

2
1 It is the heaviest weight Richard has ever lifted.
2 It is the most delicious meal I have ever eaten.
3 It is the driest summer we have ever had.
4 It was the most poisonous snake that Michael had ever handled.
5 It is the most accurate watch I have ever owned.
6 It was the most outrageous proposal John had ever heard.
7 It was the worst accident the doctor had ever been called to.
8 Jake Carter was the most dangerous criminal P.C. Smith had ever arrested.
9 It was the saddest sight I had ever seen.
10 It was the nicest birthday present that Margaret had ever received.

Reading: *My body and I* (page 11)

A Students should work in pairs or groups of three to discuss the pre-reading questions. The theme of this article is keeping fit and doing a job that helps other people. The text gives information about the life-guard that covers both personal appearance, personality traits and attitude to his work.

Elicit vocabulary items such as *to drown, to save people's lives, to be swept out to sea, to train once/twice a week, to have one or two training sessions per week.*

B Students can do this task alone, or with a partner, according to the style the teacher finds most appropriate for the group.

1 vital
2 coach
3 considerate
4 volunteer
5 irritating
6 thanks to
7 got distracted
8 funny
9 peak
10 regime
11 assess

C The comprehension exercise should be done in pairs.

1 He's of average height with a fit and powerful body.
2 He's considerate, kind and hard-working.
3 He trains them to be lifesavers.

4 He's kind and selfless.
5 He's very matter-of-fact about it.
6 He's very modest in the way he describes what he has done.
7 He saved a businessman who collapsed in the street; a woman who was having difficulty in the sea off Crete; a trainee lifesaver who sank into the water.
8 He does a range of activities – circuit training, water-polo, and competitive swimming.
9 No.
10 You must be aware of your own limitations.

Reading: *Looking good* (page 12)

A Students should be encouraged to discuss what they do to make themselves look good. The text moves on from keeping fit, as discussed in the previous text, to the idea of how you present yourself. It deals also with clothes, fashion and cosmetics.

Elicit vocabulary such as *to put on/wear make-up, to make the most of yourself, to be stylish/ trendy/ elegant, to feel good in.*

B **skin**: cleanse moisturise massage perfume

eyes: bags

hair: trim shampoo conditioner

C 1 D 2 C 3 C 4 D 5 B

Talking Points (page 13)

Section 1

The photograph shows a bee-keeper at work. Ensure that the students know the following items: *bee-keeper, a hive, make honey, to sting/a sting, protective clothing.*

Some other situations where special clothing is worn are: in the police, where the uniform allows the public to recognise authority figures; in medicine, and other areas where hygiene is important; in jobs where the body must be protected, such as pest-control, the nuclear industry, fire-fighting; in the armed forces where camouflage is important.

Section 2

Allow students the chance to express their individual choices, but make sure they are able to produce the appropriate vocabulary items such as *a uniform, a suit, a matching outfit, practical, hard-wearing, formal, sophisticated, stylish, casual, attractive, daring, fashionable.*

Section 3

Check that the students are familiar with the following phrases and can produce them naturally in context:

Can I help you?
Have you got …?
I'm looking for a …
I'll take that one.
Have you got something cheaper?
Can I have a refund?
Have you got the receipt?
Can I exchange it for …?
Have you got something smaller/more colourful?

Listening: *The clothes I wear* (page 14)

Notes on the text

The speaker comes from Scotland and speaks with a slight accent. He refers to traditional Scottish clothing:

a kilt: a short, full, pleated tartan skirt

a dress jacket: a black jacket

a skiandu: a short dagger worn in the sock

Tapescript

ALASDAIR: Well today I'm dressed quite casually I think with a sort of light green pair of cord trousers on, a polo T-shirt type of, er, of shirt, plus a black lambswool sweater and some comfortable slip-on shoes.

INTERVIEWER: Are these the sort of clothes that you'd wear if you were going to work?

ALASDAIR: Yes actually they are, because my work expects me to be quite comfortably dressed in a relaxed fashion, though within, within certain constraints of course.

INTERVIEWER: What kind of clothes are you going to wear for your wedding?

ALASDAIR: That's an interesting question, and hasn't yet been resolved. But I think I'm likely to wear a full Highland outfit which means a kilt, a dress jacket, er long woollen socks and a 'skiandu' which is a kind of short dagger worn in the sock.

INTERVIEWER: So will other members of your family be wearing the same thing?

ALASDAIR: Not if they have any sense! No. Ah it is possible. Yes some of my cousins might and maybe one or two of my uncles might. But not others, it's certainly not the convention.

INTERVIEWER: So what kind of clothes would you wear if you were going for an interview?

ALASDAIR: Oh when I have gone for interviews in the past I've always had to wear formal clothes because that's what I suppose was expected of me. And I wear suits. Practically every interview I've ever attended I've worn a suit.

INTERVIEWER: So do you have to keep a suit just for interviews?

ALASDAIR: Well, I use the suit for interviews but I suit ... I have ... I use the same suit for other occasions as well.

INTERVIEWER: What sort of occasions?

ALASDAIR: If I were going to some function perhaps, a more formal function.

INTERVIEWER: What, like a dinner party?

ALASDAIR: Probably not a dinner party because the dinner parties I go to tend to be more jacket and tie, and, and erm, pair of flannels perhaps. But erm if I were going to a Christmas party, perhaps at work where everybody was dressing up for the occasion, then perhaps I'd wear that.

A
1. light green
2. cord
3. a polo T-shirt
4. (lambs)wool
5. comfortable clothes
6. a Highland outfit with a kilt, dress jacket, special socks and a dagger
7. for an interview; for something like a dinner or Christmas party where everybody dresses up

Notes on the text

The speaker refers to two well-known British retailers, *Marks and Spencer* and *Laura Ashley*.

Tapescript

HELEN: Well at the moment I'm wearing floral dungarees from Laura Ashley and a blue T-shirt and a men's Marks and Spencer's red cardigan.

INTERVIEWER: Aha and are these the kinds of clothes you most like to wear?

HELEN: This kind of thing? Yes, yes, I like to wear casual, comfortable clothes really.

INTERVIEWER: Right. So these are the clothes you would wear for work?

HELEN: Well, probably yes, because I, I, I teach, and I teach at home and er I probably would wear this sort of thing for work.

INTERVIEWER: When would you wear something rather more formal?

HELEN: Well, probably if I were working, erm working elsewhere. I mean occasionally I, I go out to work and I might put on a skirt for instance. Or if I'm going out to dinner and it's a fairly formal dinner party. I would wear something more formal then.

INTERVIEWER: So generally speaking, do you prefer wearing trousers to wearing skirts?

HELEN: Yes I do. Yes, yes I do.

INTERVIEWER: I mean, can you explain why this is? Is it just that they're more convenient?

HELEN: Well it's because they're more convenient

and because the shoes that you wear with trousers are usually much more comfortable, and erm, because skirts involve finding a pair of tights that isn't laddered. And finding a pair of shoes that the heels are vaguely respectable. And that kind of thing. I find, I find dressing smartly rather a strain to be perfectly honest.

INTERVIEWER: Right, so what sort of clothes would you wear for an interview then?

HELEN: Oh, well, I would make a real effort I think for an interview. Because I think it's important to look as if you've made an effort. Because of, of the impression that gives, so probably I would wear quite a smart skirt or even a, even a dress. I'd probably buy things specially, actually if it was for an interview, if it was important.

B
1 b,e trousers – relaxing, working at home
2 a, c, d skirt – interview, dinner party, working away from home
3 a dress – interview
4 b, e comfortable shoes – relaxing, working at home
5 a, c, d tights – interview, dinner party, working away from home
6 a something bought especially for the occasion – interview

Writing: *Describing people* (page 14)

A Most descriptions of people tend to move from general factual details concerning appearance to more subjective opinions on character.

English in Use (page 15)

1 Finding errors

1 *the* is incorrect
2 *been* is incorrect
3 *object to helping* is correct, *to* in *mind helping* is incorrect, *out* is incorrect in the last sentence.
4 *more* is incorrect
5 *it* is incorrect; second sentence is correct
6 *been* is incorrect
7 *lot* is incorrect
8 sentence is correct
9 *upper* is incorrect

2 Word-formation

1 impolite
2 unsuitable
3 unreliable
4 impractical
5 unexpected

unit 2 A PLACE OF YOUR OWN

Lead-in (page 16)

1 Ask students to look at the pictures and discuss the questions in pairs or small groups, using the words given.

The top photograph is a natural landscape showing a rural village which is probably both peaceful and quiet. It seems to be a farming village because of the gate which might lead to fields with crops in them. (The photograph is actually of a village in Gloucestershire, England.) The bottom photograph is a typical shot of a busy high street in a city. There is a lot of traffic and many pedestrians. It seems quite noisy but with a lively atmosphere. The architecture of the building at the end of the street is grand and imposing. (The photograph is actually Liverpool City Centre.)

2

1	q	11	h
2	d	12	j
3	t	13	s
4	g	14	l
5	p	15	r
6	k	16	m
7	n	17	c
8	i	18	f
9	b	19	e
10	o	20	a

3 Pre-teach the words given, as necessary. This exercise is not a test but an opportunity to learn and practise the vocabulary which is relevant to the unit and which occurs in the reading passages.

Make sure that students read the text to the end before starting to complete it. Ask students to compare their answers when they finish. Students can also practise giving an oral summary of the text.

1	doorstep	9	lack
2	major city	10	social life
3	amenities	11	gossip
4	leisure activities	12	home background
5	drawbacks	13	on campus
6	crime-rate	14	facilities
7	cost of living	15	live
8	beautiful scenery		

Reading: *Doing up a derelict house* (page 18)

A In Britain there is a tendency to prefer old houses to new ones, which may be quite different from the attitude in other countries. The reason for this preference is that old houses are built of brick or stone, which can last for hundreds of years. They are usually bigger than new housing and often contain features, such as fireplaces, doors and plasterwork, made from valuable materials by skilful craftsmen, which would be expensive to put in a new house. 'Do It Yourself' is also very popular in Britain, so many people are willing to restore an old house. Quite a few people build their own houses on land they have bought, either alone or in small groups, even if they have not had any previous building experience. Here is a chance to explore different attitudes to housing.

B
1 a very small cramped flat near or in the centre of a city
2 almost a ruin
3 impossible to live in
4 very pleased to sell the houses at last
5 from the beginning
6 connect the house to gas, electricity and water supplies
7 the completed work that they have done
8 a very overgrown area of land where plants have gone completely wild

C
1 Their city flat was very small and they wanted to live in the country.
2 Any four of the following: the tiles had slipped off the roof, the gutters were hanging down, most windows were broken, doors were hanging off, several floorboards were rotten, birds had built nests and there was a tree inside one of the houses.
3 The houses were in such a bad condition.
4 The view was idyllic.
5 The owner didn't expect that anyone would want to buy them.
6 They made the three cottages into one, they rebuilt an end wall, they connected the house to gas, water and electricity supplies.
7 One.
8 The outside.
9 He advised them to knock down the original end wall and build it up again on new foundations.
10 They still have to make a new garden.

Grammar: *past simple, present perfect* (Grammar Notes **2.1** and **7.1**) (page 19)

A
1 a Did John's plane leave on time?
b Yes, it did. But the airline refused to take one of his bags so I've brought it back here. What shall we do with it?
2 a The police haven't found the money yet, have they?
b No, the robbers hid it straight after the robbery and so far none of them has said where it is.
3 a Have you seen Elizabeth recently?
b No, I haven't. We met for lunch three weeks ago but I haven't seen her since.
4 a What did Jack do with the letter when you gave it to him?
b He said nothing and then tore it into tiny pieces.
5 a Has the coach chosen Michael for next Saturday's team?
b I haven't seen the list yet but he did/didn't last time.
6 a How many races has this horse won?
b Four so far this year, plus the ten he won last year. He hasn't lost any yet.
7 a Have you eaten in this café before?
b No, but I ate a lot of Italian food when I was on holiday there last year. Have you ever been there?

B Make sure that students identify the three sentences for which a past simple form is not possible before they complete the other sentences. The three sentences are:

2 … have been friends since they were at university (present perfect).
5 … have lived/have been living in this house for twenty years (present perfect *or* present perfect continuous).
8 was planting rose-bushes … (past continuous).

1 bought
3 froze
4 lived
6 vanished/disappeared/went away/left
7 mend/repair/fix, did
9 grew/ate
10 met

C This exercise is designed to practise the question form of the past simple. It is most important that students can form questions correctly. Mistakes of the 'Where he went?' type are still quite common at this level. Make sure students realise that 'did' is needed in every sentence and that their questions are directed to Mr Campbell, so they should use the pronoun 'you'. It is best to do pair practice after you have checked that the written answers are correct. During pair practice students can think of additional questions to ask.

3 Where did you go after leaving home?
4 When/what time did you return home?
5 What did you see first of all?
6 How did you know something was wrong?
7 When did you call the police?
8 Did you speak to anyone else?
9 Why did the burglars choose your house?
10 What did the burglars steal?

Listening: *A good crop* (page 20)

Tapescript

INTERVIEWER: Erm, have you got a garden?

ANTHONY: Yes, yes, yes I've got quite a big, erm, garden and erm, well I'm very fond of my garden. I, I, I spend a lot of time in it and I grow a lot of things. Erm … there is the small garden at the front but the main garden's at the back of the house. And erm, just right next to the house there's a patio which is built of bricks laid on the ground and then after the patio there's a lawn and on the lawn there's a climbing frame for, for the children. As you're on the patio there's a wooden bench and there's also a kind of picnic table which we use quite a lot in summer because it means we can eat outside. And then to the left of the lawn there's a brick path which goes … not in a straight line but in a kind of curving, it curves towards the shed at the end of the garden. And then the lawn's to the right of the path. And to the left of it there's a small, erm well, there's a kind of herb, herb garden and some rose bushes and there's also a, a compost bin where we put all the rubbish. And then after the lawn towards the end of the garden there are, erm vegetable plots where I grow vegetables. And I've divided it into about oh, three, five, five different vegetable plots. And the reason I've got five is that so that I can rotate the vegetables from year to year. But erm, I grow quite a lot of vegetables … I mean this, this year for example, I've grown a lot of potatoes. In fact I've grown er five different varieties of potato. And I had a very good crop of er peas. And I also grew beans, and er a lot of garlic. An excellent crop of garlic. I grow garlic every year. It's very, very easy to grow.

INTERVIEWER: Do you use fertilisers and things?

ANTHONY: Well I use, I use the compost from the compost bin. Erm, erm I, I put that on the garden and dig it in. But I don't use any chemicals. I use some organic fertilisers.

For example I use a fertiliser which is called erm, blood, hoof and horn which is a sort of natural, organic fertiliser, plus the compost but I don't use any chemicals. And erm I also grew … some, some pumpkins. I had quite a good crop of pumpkins and erm what else? Erm … well carrots. Carrots were quite good this year. I had a good crop of carrots. And a few onions but they, not … they weren't so good this year to be honest. And erm lettuce, I always grow lettuce. I mean they're easy to grow. I had quite a good crop of lettuce. And also cucumber and spring onions. I had quite a good crop of spring onions, and erm that's about it really. I mean each year I try and grow a different kind of vegetable … something I haven't tried before. But erm usually I get … I get a lot of vegetables from the garden. Certainly during the … during the summer I mean from about erm May to, say er October, most of the vegetables that we eat are from the garden.

A These vegetables are mentioned: 1, 3, 4, 5, 7, 8, 10, 11, 12, 14.

B The path doesn't curve, there are only three rows of vegetables, there is no climbing frame on the lawn, there is no picnic table on the patio, there are no rose bushes, there is no compost bin.

English in Use: *prepositions, household vocabulary* (page 20)

1

1	on	6	with, on
2	round	7	at, at
3	on	8	into
4	with	9	in, next
5	At	10	with

2

1 a tree-lined avenue
2 an architect-designed house
3 a centrally heated house
4 a well-ventilated kitchen
5 a timber-framed house
6 a well-situated house

3 Containers and contents

1 G	6 D
2 A	7 H
3 E	8 J
4 F	9 C
5 B	10 I

Reading: *A room of my own* (page 21)

A Ask students to work in pairs or small groups. If students have never looked for a place to live themselves ask them to think of other people who have.

B

1	threadbare	7	a rug
2	shabby	8	gloomy
3	despaired	9	coats
4	a dump	10	stank
5	strictly speaking	11	sprinkling
6	mean		

C 1 B – phoning and finding places had already gone, visiting flats and finding they were dark and poky, finding that landlords were strange.
2 A
3 B
4 B – buying a rug, painting the walls.

Reading: *My favourite village* (page 22)

A In this passage the author remembers a village where he would often go on holiday when he was young.

Answer the pre-reading questions eliciting vocabulary such as *I remember … with affection/with terror, to feel/be nostalgic about something, to remind you of something.*

B

1	picturesque	8	winding
2	idyllic	9	weep
3	peace and quiet	10	brook
4	nostalgic	11	incredible vibrancy
5	creep	12	swamped
6	acquired	13	magic
7	stock up with	14	drabber

C
1 False. He only likes villages for short visits.
2 False. Platres is high up in the mountains.
3 True.
4 True.
5 False. The journey on the winding roads made him feel sick.
6 False. The main difference was that it was cooler.
7 False. The children got on very well – the 'fighting' was just a game.
8 False. Only the writer's friend was punished.
9 False. The writer's aunt stayed with them many times – '*she used to come*'.
10 True. (It is still very popular but seems less attractive to the writer.)

Talking Points (page 23)

Section 1

Students should use the words given to describe the photographs.

The top photograph shows a detached house, a country cottage made of brick and painted white. It has a tiled porch and roses climbing up the walls. There is a garden path leading to the front door and there are some well-kept flowerbeds and a lawn lining the path. The bottom photograph shows a semi-detached house, a town house made of brick with white painted windowsills. There are bay windows and the attic looks as if it has been converted into a bedroom. The front garden has a lawn on one side and some shrubs on the other and is surrounded by a brick wall.

Section 2

Ensure that students know and can produce vocabulary for all the rooms in a house. Students should begin by talking about the layout of the flat and its suitability for living alone, living as a couple, and living with a friend or with family. Continue on to Section 3 in which the discussion should broaden out and students no longer need support from the pictures and plans. It is important to do this in small groups so that there is an opportunity for agreement and disagreement.

Listening: *My own place* (page 24)

Tapescript

1 DAVID: The first thing I have to say about the house I live in is that it's deceptive. In fact, when people come in they say, 'Gosh this house is deceptive, isn't it?' It's erm, it's an end of terrace, Victorian cottage and it looks quite small from the outside but in fact er, inside it's quite large because we've added to it ... a bit like a building kit. You know we've put on a kitchen and we've put on a dining room and er, now recently we've put another bedroom in the loft upstairs. So it has, I suppose, one very large sitting-room, a large kitchen erm, with a dining-room attachment and then it has now four bedrooms. Although the third bedroom I tend to call my study and everybody else calls an office. It does look a bit like an office really more than a study. And I don't study in there so that's not erm a particularly accurate description of it. And then there's, erm, a new bedroom upstairs with its bathroom attached. So in fact it's a four-bedroomed house with a large lounge and a kitchen.

1
1 They say, 'Gosh, this house is deceptive, isn't it?'
2 It is bigger inside than it seems to be when seen from the outside.
3 It had one room downstairs and three bedrooms (and probably one bathroom although this isn't mentioned explicitly).
4 He has added a kitchen, a dining room and a fourth bedroom with a bathroom.
5 An office (or a study).

Notes on the text

lumberjack: someone whose job is to cut down trees

tied cottage: a house which is rented out by the employer to someone who works on his/her land

Tapescript

2 ALASDAIR: I was brought up in the Highlands of Scotland near a town called Fort William which is known really only because of its heavy rainfall, because it er, it also has the highest mountain in Great Britain, called Ben Nevis. And I lived twenty miles from there in a little village called South Lagan, which is a village tied to a, a forestry community really. That's what my father did. He worked as a … he worked as a lumberjack in the Forestry Commission and he had a tied cottage which was also a small farm, a croft. And I lived there until … until I went to Glasgow at the age of eighteen … very remote, well no, I wouldn't say it was very remote … it's certainly quite remote in most people's understanding of the word, though our nearest town is, as I say, erm Fort William twenty miles away, or Inverness forty miles away. And I went to a little school there, with twelve, or when I left, twelve er pupils at the school … which has now, er subsequently closed.

2
1. It's famous for heavy rainfall and the highest mountain in Great Britain, Ben Nevis.
2. Twenty miles and forty miles.
3. A lumberjack – he worked for the Forestry Commission.
4. When he was eighteen.
5. Twelve.
6. It has closed.

Writing: *Letter to a friend* (page 24)

Students should follow the pattern of the example letter closely.

English in Use (page 24)

1 **A** Phrasal verbs

In this exercise *up* conveys a more emphatic meaning in every case.

1. Speak (speak more loudly)
2. Eat (eat everything)
3. Lock (lock securely)
4. Drink (finish your drinks)
5. Stand (get to your feet)

B 1 d 2 a 3 b 4 e 5 c

C In this exercise there are more examples of how the particle can modify the meaning of the verb.

1. *tired out* means 'completely tired'. It is stronger than 'I'm tired'.
2. *beaten up* means hit several times with fists and feet and injured very badly. By itself, 'beaten' also implies to hit many times but with an object such as an iron bar or stick. A common expression is 'beaten to death'. 'Beaten up' cannot be followed by 'with a stick' or 'to death'.
3. *spell it out* means 'say each letter aloud', so that the word can be written down by another person.
4. *read it out* means 'read it aloud'.
5. *count it out* means to count the coins slowly and obviously, perhaps putting them into the hand of another person, or counting aloud.

D *Pick* when applied to fruit, vegetables and flowers means to separate them from the bush or tree on which they are growing or to break the stem. If we *pick* them *up*, they have already fallen from the tree.

Grow can be used about people and plants because it means to increase in physical size. *Grow up* means to become like an adult in manner and behaviour and can therefore only be used about people.

1. have grown
2. picked
3. grow
4. Pick up
5. grew up

2 Countable, uncountable nouns (Grammar Notes **2.2**)

A **Normally countable:** people, feet, children, teeth, sheep, mice.
Normally uncountable: news, information, luggage, money, luck, spaghetti (NB in many European languages this is a plural countable noun), traffic, advice.

B

1	much	7	much
2	many	8	much
3	much	9	many
4	much	10	much
5	much	11	many
6	many	12	much

3 Word-formation

1	widening	6	straighten
2	modernise	7	itemises/itemised
3	sharpening	8	strengthened
4	economise	9	generalise
5	deafening	10	lengthen

unit 3 MAKING A NEW START

Lead-in (page 26)

1 This unit deals with changes in people's lives, and the students need to consider the advantages and disadvantages that such events bring about. The lead-in pictures focus on areas that are likely to be either within the life experience of young students (moving house – photograph below) or about to happen to them (enrolling at college – photograph above).

Students should work in pairs or groups of three to discuss the photographs and reactions to major change. Useful adjectives to describe feelings are *excited, eager, keen, sad, nervous, anxious, curious, apprehensive*; to describe changes are *leaving old friends, meeting new people, adapting to a new environment, settling down, getting to know people, developing relationships, meeting new challenges, adjusting to a different timetable/ different social life, getting used to things.*

2

1	making	6	inherited
2	settle down	7	lottery
3	feel at home	8	widen
4	redundant	9	mature
5	refugees	10	lifestyle

3

1	dismissed	6	released
2	dropped	7	leave
3	deported	8	expel
4	evicted	9	evacuated
5	discharged	10	retired

Reading: *A change for the better* (page 28)

A Students should discuss the pre-reading questions in pairs or small groups leading on to a class discussion of everyone's responses. Encourage students to explore the subject area of change and relate it to their own experience. They can discuss different reactions to moving house and major upheaval such as *excitement, stress* and *apprehension.*

Notes on the text

civil servant: a government employee (but not teachers)

suburb: an area on the outskirts of town

semi-detached: a house joined to the house next door by a shared wall e.g. *The Smiths live in a small semi-detached house.*

loch: a lake in Scotland

refurbish: a formal word meaning to clean and decorate a building

B 1 G 2 A 3 I 4 D 5 B 6 H 7 E

Grammar: *past continuous, past simple* (Grammar Notes **2.1**, **3.1**) (page 29)

A 1 a What was Sarah doing when you went to her house?
b She was writing a report but she stopped doing that and we went out for a meal.
2 a What was John doing when you phoned him?
b I don't know but he stopped whatever he was doing and came round to my house

immediately.

3 a How long were you rehearsing the play last night?
  b Until 10 p.m. but the director thought we weren't making much progress so we decided to stop.

4 a Did the police arrest Jack at his hotel?
  b No, later when he was waiting for a train.

5 a Were the others still working when you left the office?
  b Yes, they were. I went back after an hour and we worked until 10 p.m.

B Make sure that students understand that it is the order of the actions that matters, not the order of the verbs in the sentence.

1 was looking, found
2 was checking, spotted
3 was skating, gave way
4 twisted, was playing
5 was driving, overtook
6 was visiting, met
7 was sunbathing, hit
8 was making, threw
9 cut, was peeling
10 stole, was watching
11 was running, shot

Listening: *Going to university* (page 30)

Tapescript

INTERVIEWER: Erm, I know the next twelve months are going to be very important for you. What do you think … what do you hope will happen in the next twelve months?

CLAIRE: Well I hope that in the next few weeks, I have my mock exams, and I hope that I prepare myself for them correctly, properly and efficiently and get pretty good results erm …

INTERVIEWER: So is it really important for you to get good results?

CLAIRE: Yes, I think so because that would boost my confidence but also if I don't get the good results then I can think, 'well, I've got to work harder', and it'll make me more concentrated on doing it but if I do get good results then that will be an added bonus!

INTERVIEWER: Right. And when are the actual exams that you have to take?

CLAIRE: The actual exams I think are in June which … I mean it seems quite a long way away now but I'm sure they'll come incredibly quickly so, I'm taking Biology, Chemistry and Physics, so between now and then I will really just be preparing for those exams – erm hopefully quite intensively.

INTERVIEWER: What about interviews? Are you going to have interviews?

CLAIRE: I hope so.

INTERVIEWER: And you'll get an invitation directly from the university will you?

CLAIRE: Yes.

INTERVIEWER: Right. What is it you want to study at university?

CLAIRE: I'd really, really love to study Veterinary Science.

INTERVIEWER: And is it very, very difficult to get places on these courses?

CLAIRE: Yes. It's very, very difficult because the competition is just so high, erm I think the statistics are there's something like 75 people apply for one place and there's something like erm 300 places in the country.

INTERVIEWER: So what have you done to try and maximise your chances of being offered a place?

CLAIRE: I've done an awful lot of work experience in a veterinary practice; I've done work experience on farms with sheep, erm and horses; I've worked in a livery yard; erm I've owned my own horse and all these things benefit me a great deal but, provided they read my reference of course, they will see that and hopefully offer me a place.

INTERVIEWER: And how many years would it take for you to get qualified if you got accepted on the course?

CLAIRE: Five years provided I passed each year.

1 Veterinary Science
2 five years
3 Biology
4 Chemistry } (in any order)
5 Physics

Previous experience: yes, with sheep and horses

English in Use (page 30)

1 (Grammar Notes **3.2**)

1	waiting for	5	expect
2	expecting	6	hope
3	hoping	7	expects
4	hope, expect	8	looking forward to

2 (Grammar Notes **3.3**)

1	earn	5	gain
2	won	6	win
3	gain	7	gained
4	won	8	earn

3 (Grammar Notes **3.4**)

1	am … used to	6	are … used to
2	get used to	7	get used to
3	get used to	8	will … get used to
4	got used to	9	get used to
5	was used to	10	were … used to

Reading: *Looking forward to the time of our lives* (page 31)

The reading text relates five people's expectations of leaving home and going to university. Ask students to work in pairs and discuss their experiences of moving away from home and/or leaving secondary school. If the students in your class are younger than school-leaving age ask them to outline their expectations and compare their own with those given in the text. Which person's expectations, expressed in the reading passage, are nearest to their own?

A The text is followed by a matching exercise that involves scanning the text for the information.

Notes on the text

a degree: the usual way of referring to a BA (Bachelor of Arts) or BSc (Bachelor of Science), which are qualifications awarded in British universities

Oxford: one of Britain's oldest universities, and one of the most prestigious; people who are students at Oxford belong to a college of the university

comprehensive school: a State secondary school for pupils from the age of 11 to 16 (the school-leaving age) or 18

public school: a private school at secondary level, for which parents of students must pay; attended by 5% of the school population in Britain

a nine-to-five job: the phrase used to cover routine office jobs

a vocational degree: a degree immediately relevant to the work you intend to do afterwards, such as a degree in law, medicine or education

Interrail: a railway ticket that provides unlimited travel on certain European railways for one month. Often used as a verb: *'What did you do in the summer?' 'I went interrailing.'*

B

1	A, C, D, E	5	C, E
2	A	6	A, B, D, E
3	A, C	7	B
4	C, D, E	8	B, D

Reading: *The worst of times* (page 32)

A *Notes on the text*

The text is written in a colloquial style. Note the number of words in the text that are negative: *bitter*, *resentful*, *ostracised*, *bullied*, *revulsion*.

shrink: a colloquial word for a psychiatrist

B

1	paralysed	7	revulsion
2	a real struggle	8	convinced
3	distressed	9	shoplifting
4	resentful	10	show off
5	ostracised	11	humiliating
6	bullied	12	sane

C
1. She liked it.
2. She had an operation that went wrong and it left her paralysed and unable to speak.
3. Her father's job took her there.
4. Thirteen.
5. Yes, she was.
6. Her boyfriend.
7. She was made to feel unwelcome.
8. She was self-conscious about the fact that she was getting fat.
9. She was no longer part of the group she had belonged to and her boyfriend wasn't friendly.
10. She stole cosmetics from a shop.

Talking Points (page 33)

Section 1

In Britain, the football pools are a way in which people have the chance of winning a large sum of money by predicting the results of football matches. The photograph shows a woman receiving a cheque for £2,072,200 from Littlewoods' football pools. The changes to come will, no doubt, be drastic for her. In fact many companies in Britain, which run football pools, give their winners free financial advice on how to cope with and invest their money, how to cope with their own changes of expectations in life, and what possibilities the future can hold.

Students should discuss their reactions to sudden changes in fortune, especially suddenly receiving a large sum of money.

Section 2

Not all changes are positive, and students are here provided with the chance to discuss stress factors. Stress arising from change is obviously handled differently by different people but the most commonly cited causes of stress are *the death of a close relative, breaking up with a partner, changing your job, getting married* and *moving to a new house.*

Elicit the following vocabulary from students such as *lonely, strange, excited, making decisions, adapting yourself, upset, distressed, an outsider, difficult to get used to, to come to terms with.*

Listening: *Immigrants* (page 34)

Tapescript

Ellis Island is a small windswept island in the harbour of New York City. Nothing special about that, you might think, but between the years of 1892 and 1931 over twelve million immigrants, most of whom were from Europe, passed through the island before starting their new lives as citizens of the United States.

A museum has recently been opened on the island, and this allows today's generation of young Americans to relive the experiences of their ancestors. It's a fact that some 40 per cent of American citizens have ancestors who passed through immigration at the island, and this includes some of the most famous. They arrived in New York City having made the journey from Europe in crowded uncomfortable ships and were then taken across the harbour in ferries to be processed by the Immigration Authorities. A building was opened on the island in 1900 to handle the processing of half a million immigrant arrivals a year. By 1907, the year when it dealt with the greatest number of applicants, nearly 900,000 immigrants passed through the building. Visitors to the island today can re-live all the difficulties and hardships of this experience by watching a short film, 'The Island of Hope, Island of Tears' which shows what happened to immigrants when they got to Ellis Island.

The immigrants who came to the island were those who had travelled on ship in the cheapest accommodation available. The wealthier travellers were dealt with quickly in New York. The Ellis Island immigrants entered the building through a glass and metal porch and passed first into the baggage hall where they had to deposit all their belongings. Giuseppe Santi was so impressed that he later told his grandchildren: 'If they let the poor into such a gorgeous hall, I knew it was possible to be rich in America.' Next the immigrants had to walk up a huge staircase for a medical examination. This could be a terrifying experience, because those found to have certain diseases were not allowed to stay in the United States. If they tripped on the staircase, the doctors might mark their coats with an 'E' for eye-disease. If they were out of breath, they could be marked with an 'H' for heart-disease.

The next test came in the Registry Room, where there were more questions from officials. If an immigrant failed to satisfy the inspectors with their answers, they were sent to a special inquiry room for more questioning. Some two per cent of immigrants were sent back home for failing to provide adequate answers. Now visitors to the museum can hear how immigrants felt about all these frightening experiences, by listening to tape recordings made by them now as they look back on the events of many years ago.

Not all the experiences on Ellis Island were negative. Some immigrants remember their first experiences of eating ice-cream or tasting bananas. One young boy loved the hot water shower so much that he recalls on the tape how he began to sing.

There's lots to see on the island, as there are over 30 separate galleries containing objects associated with the immigrants – things like posters, photos and maps – and there is a 'Treasures from Home' room with clothes, jewellery and religious articles brought by the immigrants to their new home in the States and now donated to the Museum.

If you want to visit Ellis Island, it's an all-day excursion from New York City. You take the ferry from Battery Park via the Statue of Liberty. Food is available on the ferry, or you can eat on an outside terrace on the island and enjoy a spectacular view of the New York skyline at the same time.

1 C 2 C 3 C 4 C 5 D

Writing: *Telling a story* (page 34)

The instructions in the Students' Book give clear guidelines to the students, but in assessing students' compositions teachers should consider not only how coherent the storyline is, but also provide feedback to the students about the need for a tight focus, i.e. in this case the need to talk about *one* event, happening on *one* day, and the *various* effects on your life both then and now.

English in Use (page 35)

1

1	got	7	were
2	in	8	way
3	waiting	9	who
4	course	10	same
5	career	11	as
6	like	12	required
13	with	17	number
14	relevant	18	had/attended
15	could	19	if
16	any	20	out

2 Phrasal verbs

1	set up	6	set off/out
2	set in	7	set/sets down
3	set out	8	set off
4	set off/out	9	set on
5	set about	10	set/sets … apart

3 Word-formation

1	investigator	6	murderer
2	workers	7	directors
3	suppliers	8	beggars
4	operator	9	translator
5	navigator	10	Robbers

unit 4 GETTING ABOUT

Lead-in (page 36)

1 This unit deals with various ways of travelling: *by car, by train, on foot*, etc. Discussion of the photos and lead-in questions can be done in pairs or small groups or you can elicit vocabulary and ideas and build them up on the board. You can build up lists of pleasures, excitement, discomforts and dangers associated with the forms of travel shown in the photographs. At this stage you should listen for and correct mistakes of the 'I went on a travel' kind. Point out to students that 'travel' cannot be used with an indefinite article. If they need to talk about a particular piece of 'travel' they should use another word like *journey*, or *trip*.

The photographs show some unusual forms of travel: space travel, travelling in snowy conditions with a sledge and a team of huskies, and travelling in a hot-air balloon.

These two exercises deal with basic vocabulary for cars and travel generally. Students should do them individually but ask them to compare their answers, working in pairs. This will highlight any particular difficulties and speed up correction.

2

1 on	6 take
2 by	7 take off, boarded
3 ride	8 land
4 catch	9 journey
5 drive	10 trip

3

a	b
1 bonnet	1 steering-wheel
2 sun-roof	2 handbrake
3 windscreen	3 accelerator
4 headlights	4 fuel gauge
5 wheel	5 speedometer
6 number plate	6 gear stick

Reading: *Friday night burnout* (page 38)

A It is a good idea to bring in some pictures of different types of car and to discuss what sort of people drive them and what sort of image the car has. 'Burnout' means accelerating so fast that burnt rubber from the tyres is left on the road.

Notes on the text

stripped: to remove parts from a car that can be sold easily

3,000 people were killed: the population of Australia is 13 million, so 3,000 deaths is a comparatively high number. The population of the UK is 56 million and there are 6,000 deaths per year

custom-built (short form for 'customised'): changed to make the car look special and unusual

V8: this means that the engine has eight cylinders

I turn heads: the way I drive makes people turn their heads and look at me

B 1 F 2 B 3 E 4 A 5 D

Grammar: *ways of talking about the future* (Grammar Notes **4.1**) (page 39)

1 b, c	9 b, c
2 a	10 b
3 a	11 a
4 b	12 a, c
5 a, c	13 b
6 b	14 a
7 a	15 b, c
8 b	

Listening: *An incident on the motorway* (page 40)

Notes on the text

The speaker says '30 or 40 feet' but he must mean '30 or 40 inches' or even '3 or 4 inches'. In the context of an exciting story, neither the speaker nor the listeners may notice such slips of the tongue.

old banger: a very old car

Tapescript

JAMES: While I was travelling down to er, Farnham, which is only 50 or 60 miles away, er just early one evening in a flow of rush-hour traffic, very, very heavy I think it was on a Friday, with a friend of mine, driving down in my old banger, my old car and er … (this is when I had a car, I had to sell it because er, in the end, when I … and you'll soon see why). I er you know were travelling down and the actual lanes on this motorway erm, are very … were very narrow and, heavy rush-hour traffic, and er, I was driving along and I knew the brakes needed a bit of attention, really. But erm … anyway we were going along very … chatting away you know, as you do in a car you know, with a long journey and er … I was in, I got into the fast lane and the cars were going side, side by side really, you know only about, maybe 30 or 40 feet apart and I suddenly saw this, this gap opened up, so I swerved into the lane and I really started to motor and I was chatting away and then I suddenly realised that I was getting very close to the car in front and I thought, 'That car has stopped!' and as I thought 'That car has stopped,' I thought, 'Put your foot on the brake,' and I put my foot on the brake and nothing happened. Nothing happened. And I saw the ... this, the front, the back of the car in front getting closer and closer and closer and closer and just as I was about to hit the car in front and my foot was on the brake I thought, 'Turn!' and I turned the steering wheel left ... it's a miracle how I didn't hit a car to my left, there was a space to my left, and I literally ... I just heard this slight tinkle as I missed the car in front of me by, I mean it must have been about a matter of about two feet. I missed it, and I heard a tinkle to my right and I looked to my right, I'd almost let go of the steering wheel in shock and I looked to my right and the ... erm ... my right wing mirror had been smashed, and that was all. Nothing else on the car had been touched so it had literally been a matter of about two or three inches.

1 False. He was driving in the evening.
2 False. There was a lot of traffic.
3 True.
4 True.
5 False. He had to sell it after the incident.
6 True.
7 False. He was with a friend.
8 True.
9 True.
10 False. His brakes failed.
11 False. His right wing mirror was smashed.

English in Use (page 40)

1 other, another, others, the others (Grammar Notes 4.2)

1 another
2 the other
3 the other
4 The others
5 Other
6 the other
7 the other
8 other
9 other
10 Others ('The others' is also possible if he means his colleagues rather than scientists in general)

2 Journey, travel (Grammar Notes 4.3)

1	cruise	6	trip
2	Travels	7	travel
3	Travel, travel	8	voyage
4	pilgrimage	9	journey
5	flight	10	journey

Reading: *The rails that narrow the mind* (page 41)

A The title is a play on the saying 'Travel broadens the mind'. The writer is very sceptical about the value of young people travelling in this way. Make sure that students grasp this point. They may disagree.

Notes on the text

backpack: the American term for rucksack NB: the noun *a backpacker* exists but *a rucksacker* does not.

hard core backpackers: really serious, dedicated and determined travellers, who never pay for a couchette

British Grand Prix: a motor-race

B 1 C 2 B 3 A 4 D 5 B

Reading: *Taking the wrong path* (page 42)

A So far the reading texts have been about cars and trains. This one is about walking. This is a good time to revise the expressions 'by car, by train etc.' but 'on foot, on horseback'.

You can elicit vocabulary associated with this activity, such as *cagoule, anorak, compass, rucksack, boots, first-aid kit,* things people often take with them when they go walking, such as *a packed lunch, a hat to protect themselves from both the sun and wind, a map.* Encourage the students to say why people might like walking such as *getting away from city/work life, being active, discovering an area, being outdoors.* Some of the dangers are *getting lost*, *breaking a limb*, *becoming exhausted*, *being bitten by insects*, *getting sunburnt*.

B

1	keen on	6	forked
2	remote	7	slope
3	well-defined	8	bothered
4	sweat	9	trudged
5	sure enough	10	quarrel

C
1 started
2 the way things were in the end
3 became smaller and smaller until it disappeared
4 understand, decide and plan

D
1 Saturday.
2 Rucksacks containing waterproof clothing, food, flasks of coffee, a torch, whistle, a map and first-aid kit.
3 No. They were wearing too many clothes and quickly began to sweat.
4 At the farm after about four kilometres.
5 What they saw from the top of the hill didn't match what was shown on the map.
6 They were cheerful and confident at the beginning, became puzzled, confused, fed up, anxious, quarrelsome and panicky by the end.
7 Still being lost when it got dark.
8 From early morning to after sunset.
9 As soon as they began the walk.
10 The compass would have told them that they were going the wrong way.

Talking Points: *The Subway Piranhas* (page 43)

Section 1

Edwin Morgan was asked to write a poem that would appear in the carriages of the Glasgow Underground. The management of the Underground decided not to use this poem.

Notes on the text

shoogling: this is a word made up by the poet to convey the movement of the train

The piranhas (a small, flesh-eating fish found in the Amazon) live under the seats of the train. They eat the passengers, who are reduced to skeletons. The transport executive then sells these skeletons to medical schools.

Listening: *Planning a Journey* (page 44)

This is essentially a note-taking exercise, and gives students an opportunity to revise and practise the language of giving directions. It leads on to the Directed Writing exercise which also involves giving directions.

Tapescript

OK then so I'll tell you how to get to my new house. You leave the motorway at junction 12 and take the road to Bedford. You know that way so I won't give you the details. Now, when you get to Bedford you go past the railway station and straight on to the second roundabout. Then you turn left and head for Rushden. You go straight on for about twenty kilometres. As you come into Rushden, look out for a pub on your right called 'The Compasses'. Take the first left turn after the pub. The sign says 'Wymington'. Go up a small hill – at the top there is a school on your left. Turn right opposite the school into Hall Avenue. Go to the end – there's a T-junction. Turn left into Manor Road and go to the end of the road and then turn right into Grangeway. My house is just past the second turning on your left. It's on the lefthand side of the road. Number 53. The garage has a red door. Have you got that or shall I go through it again?

1	twelve	9	school
2	railway station	10	T-junction
3	left	11	left
4	second	12	right
5	straight on	13	second turning
6	twenty	14	53
7	left	15	red door
8	right		

Writing: *A letter of advice* (page 44)

There are two elements to this task – giving directions and deciding what things will interest this family. There is no right answer since many solutions to the problem are possible. Links must be made between the interests of the family members and the tourist attractions.

English in Use (page 45)

1 Phrasal verbs

1	call for	5	make for
2	pulled up	6	check in
3	pick … up	7	dropping in
4	get away	8	see … off

2 So, neither (Grammar Notes **4.4**)

A 1 So did I / I didn't
2 So do I / I don't
3 So had I / I hadn't
4 Neither have I / I have
5 Neither will I / I will
6 So did I / I didn't

B 1 Neither has Sarah.
2 So would Christopher.
3 Neither could Nicholas.
4 So is Maria.
5 So would Peter.
6 So did Jenny.

3 Word-formation

1	breakable	6	advisable
2	productive	7	destructive
3	talkative	8	suitable
4	changeable	9	enjoyable
5	decisive	10	creative

unit 5 CAKES AND ALE

Lead-in (page 46)

1 The photographs show a man buying a packet of crisps in a sweet shop and a man giving a little girl some barbecued food. The barbecue is taking place outside in a park or garden.

Elicit from students a range of foods, including their favourites, such as *meat (lamb, beef), fish, vegetables, fruit, snacks.* Also ensure that students are able to reproduce the appropriate vocabulary for food for special occasions such as *a delicacy, a special treat, many courses, special preparations, good/fresh ingredients.*

2

1	balanced	8	take-away
2	lean	9	fast food
3	raw	10	instant, beans
4	tough	11	tasty
5	Root	12	pie
6	staple	13	tart
7	tender	14	bun

3

1	slice	9	main
2	mugs	10	green
3	cereal	11	vegetables
4	fillings	12	flavour
5	fruit	13	pudding
6	bar	14	heavy
7	dinner	15	go out
8	courses	16	hot

Reading: *A dinner party* (page 48)

B

1	squashed	6	salvaged
2	slice	7	exorbitant
3	couldn't be bothered	8	rinsed
4	peel	9	dashed
5	swiftly	10	at such short notice

C The things that went wrong: the tomatoes were squashed; the pot of cream burst open; she cut her finger when chopping the onions; she left some plastic wrapping on the chicken and it burnt, producing a horrible smell; she discovered she had no rice in the cupboard; she had to pay a lot of money when she bought some rice at the corner shop; she left the strawberries in her bag and forgot about them, then when she remembered, she found they were squashed; her friends phoned at the last minute and said they couldn't come to dinner.

Grammar: *Sentences with if* (Grammar Notes **5.1**) (page 49)

A There are many possible answers. The following are suggestions only.

1 If you don't hurry up …
2 If the train is on time …
3 If you take these tablets …
4 If the runner trains properly …
5 … you will improve your muscle tone.
6 … you will feel and look better.
7 … will I stand to gain.
8 … will you do the same for me tomorrow?
9 … will happen

B if + past simple + would + infinitive.

C
1 e If the rent goes up, John will leave his flat.
2 j If we don't repair it now, the roof will leak next winter.
3 i If she doesn't qualify as a doctor, what job will Sarah do?
4 f If you don't hurry up, we'll leave without you.
5 h If we refused to obey these orders, what would happen to us?
6 c If he had the money, Martin would repay the loan.
7 d If you don't let them rest, the horses will become exhausted.
8 b If I had £100,000, I would invest the money in shares.
9 g If we didn't protect it, birds would eat the fruit on the tree.
10 a If I lied to Terry, I would feel guilty.

D These are suggested answers only. There are many other possibilities.

1 If I had enough money,
2 If I had a larger garden,
3 If England were a tropical country,
4 If we drove to work,
5 it would make a lovely family home.
6 I would study art.
7 I would be able to translate this novel.
8 would he tell the police?
9 What would you pay me,
10 How would you feel,

Listening: *Being a vegetarian* (page 50)

Tapescript

INTERVIEWER: You've been a vegetarian ever since I've known you. Why is that?

HELEN: Well, you met me when I was sixteen and I think I became a vegetarian when I was fifteen which is an age where you get very fanatical about things and very identified with particular causes and I think that had a large part to play in why I became vegetarian when I was fifteen, and ever since then it's been habit more than anything else, it's erm, it's, it's a way of life, in fact, it's … I'd say it isn't an issue any more simply because I've done it for so long.

INTERVIEWER: But you must have made some sort of choice and you must feel that was the right choice otherwise you'd have changed your mind, wouldn't you?

HELEN: Yes, I think it was the right choice. I mean I'm not evangelistic about it. I'm not keen on other people being vegetarian particularly unless they want to be, I'm not bothered about that, but for me it was the right choice because, erm, I felt immediately much healthier not only physically but emotionally when I gave up eating meat because I felt that, that there was … there was something wrong in eating meat. I can't exactly put my finger on what it was because it wasn't specifically to do with cruelty to animals and it wasn't specifically to do with environmental or ecological issues but it was more to do with a kind of emotional, personal reaction to the whole idea of eating meat. And in fact I remember the moment when I decided to become vegetarian I was eating a chicken pie and I thought this is the last piece of meat I'm ever going to eat and so far it has been.

INTERVIEWER: Is there anything that you really hate eating?

KATHERINE: Yes, meat. About six or seven years ago I decided to become vegetarian although I continued to eat fish because I thought I'd feel healthier if I did and in fact I did and I lost weight. And then, occasionally I'd have the odd bacon sandwich if I felt a bit down because bacon sandwiches are one of those things that you can't really resist. But after a while I began to think that it was wrong to kill animals for, for meat, you know, to eat and then I stopped eating meat altogether and I can't say I miss it, I cook with pulses and lentils and things like that and no, I don't really miss meat at all.

1 Helen
2 Katherine
3 Katherine
4 Katherine
5 Katherine
6 Helen
7 Katherine
8 Helen
9 Helen and Katherine
10 Helen

English in Use (page 50)

1 ✓
2 in
3 like
4 either
5 ✓
6 than
7 such
8 ✓
9 of
10 on
11 ✓
12 top
13 ✓
14 you
15 of

Reading: *A Tale of Two Diets* (page 51)

A Ensure that students are able to name basic foods, such as *bread and pasta, rice, potatoes, meat, vegetables*.

Notes on the text

it stinks: a common phrase among young children to indicate they don't like something

a potato scone: a small Scottish cake

a Mars Bar icecream: an icecream with the flavour of a Mars Bar

a Toffee Crisp: a chocolate bar

cream rings: sweet cakes

a Kit Kat: a chocolate bar

Diet Coke: Coke containing a reduced number of calories

a fry-up: a meal consisting of fried food, such as eggs, bread, tomatoes

Waitrose: a supermarket

King's Road: a fashionable and affluent area of London frequented by the young

B 1 D 2 D 3 A 4 B 5 C

Reading: *Eating the Healthy Way* (page 52)

A Many people in the Western world are very conscious about what they eat.

Elicit vocabulary associated with diets such as *to go/be on a diet, to count calories, to watch your weight, to weigh yourself, to lose/put on weight.*

B **a** Ways to eat in a healthy way
eat less fat
eat less sugar
eat more fibre

b Three ways to lose weight that are mentioned are:
increase physical activity
reduce your intake of fat and sugar
increase your intake of fibre

C 1 A 2 C 3 A 4 A

D
1. Anyone who feels fatter than ideal.
2. By changing what they eat.
3. She is a qualified doctor who is putting forward views generally agreed by the medical profession.
4. One that is low in sugar and fat and high in fibre.
5. The intake of calories is greater than the energy used.
6. That they mislead people.
7. Reducing the intake of fat and sugar.
8. It provides bulk and is low in calories.

Talking Points (page 53)

Section 1

Students should be encouraged to mention exotic as well as common fruits, and use a variety of adjectives to describe them.

Vocabulary and phrases which students might need include *with a smooth/furry/prickly skin, it's juicy, it's sweet, it's a(n) summer/autumn fruit.*

Section 2

In discussing the perfect meal, students should consider not just one course, but the combination of courses, and should then go on to consider how each course is created. Make sure students know the terms for the courses: e.g. *starter, main course, side dish, dessert/pudding.* Recipes occur in the Writing section of this unit.

Listening: *In a restaurant* (page 54)

Tapescript

WOMAN: Ooh, I'm so full. It was so lovely.

MAN: God, it was wonderful.

WOMAN: Shall we have another coffee?

MAN: Oh, go on then.

WOMAN: Oh good. Are you going to ask or shall I?

MAN: No, I'll ask. Excuse me …

WOMAN: Cappuccino.

MAN: Excuse me.

WAITER: Yes.

MAN: Can we have two more coffees please …?

WOMAN: Cappuccino this time please yeah.

WAITER: You want two more coffees?

MAN: Yes please, and erm, an espresso for me.

WAITER: Excuse me just one moment please. Erm, you have settled your bill it's paid and therefore, I mean, I can't open the, the bill again.

WOMAN: Well.

WAITER: Do you understand?

WOMAN: No, we'll just have another, I mean, just, you know just add on one more coffee.

WAITER: No, I'm sorry, we need. I'm very sorry but we need this table, it's nine o'clock, we're overbooked. Can you see, there are people waiting to come in?

WOMAN: Well.

WAITER: It'll be very awkward, I mean, the paperwork involved will be, I just can't cope.

MAN: What do you mean paperwork? I don't see that this has got anything to do with …

WOMAN: Can we not give you the cash? I mean I'd just like a coffee.

WAITER: I'm sorry we do need this table; I mean you've been here now two and a half hours that's quite long enough.

WOMAN: I'm sorry. You don't normally have a time limit.

WAITER: We have people waiting to use this table. They're ready to sit down. I'm awfully sorry.

WOMAN: Can I speak to your manager please?

WAITER: No you can't. I'm quite capable of dealing with this.

MAN: I don't think you are. This is an outrageous way to talk to …

WOMAN: Can you bring two coffees right now?

WAITER: No.

WOMAN: Can you go and get the manager?

WAITER: No you cannot have coffees now. Your bill has been settled, will you please go …?

1 Another cup of coffee each (one wants a cappuccino, the other an espresso).
2 That it's already been paid.
3 The restaurant is overbooked and there are people waiting for the table.
4 No.
5 Yes, very much.
6 No.
7 They ask to see the manager, but in the end they have to leave.

A **Writing:** *Letter to a friend* (page 54)

Students should first sort out the recipes, and be made aware of specific features of recipe language, such as the use of the imperative and the clear and explicit nature of the instructions. They should then incorporate this knowledge into a letter.

Recipe 1

1 First line a cake tin.
4 Wash and dry currants, sultanas and raisins. Halve the cherries. Stir into the fruit with peel.
6 In separate bowls, sift flour and spices, then cream together butter, sugar and rind.
3 Beat the eggs into the creamed mixture a little at a time.
8 Fold in half the flour then add the dried fruit and almonds.
9 Spoon into a tin. Cook on a baking sheet in an oven pre-heated to 150˚C.
10 Check if it is ready by inserting a skewer into the centre. When the skewer comes out clean, the cake is ready.

Suggested title: Fruit cake.

Recipe 2

11 First, finely chop the onion and cut the beans into thirds.
12 Then heat the olive oil and add the crushed garlic.
2 Add the chicken pieces a few at a time and brown on all sides.
13 Remove from the pan. Drain off the fat and reserve a small quantity of the liquid.
5 Stir the onion and herbs into the pan. Add the flour, followed by the stock and the beans.
14 Bring to the boil and pour over the chicken.
7 Add the bay leaf and the seasoning to the chicken. Cover and cook at 180˚C for about an hour. Serve with boiled new potatoes.

Suggested title: Chicken casserole.

Your instructions should be clear and precise.

B The imperative is used.

English in Use (page 55)

1

1	on, of	10	from
2	in	11	to, with
3	in/for	12	into
4	on, as	13	until
5	from	14	in
6	in	15	in
7	in	16	in, to
8	on	17	from
9	under	18	on

2 Phrasal verbs

1	brings back	6	brought back
2	bring round	7	brought about
3	brought out	8	bring down
4	brought up	9	brought off
5	brought on	10	bring out

3 Word-formation

1	proposal	6	offence
2	preferences	7	disturbances
3	annoyance	8	refusal
4	approval	9	differences
5	insurance	10	correspondence

Exam Practice 1 (page 56)

1 1 F 2 B 3 E 4 G 5 A 6 H 7 D

2

1	wherever/where/ anywhere	8	for
		9	a
2	make	10	less
3	which/that	11	do
4	there	12	to
5	its	13	with/to
6	in	14	would
7	this/that	15	no

3

1 Elizabeth and Susan both share/have the same birthday.
2 He gave me hardly any information/details about his research project.
3 Please give me some advice on the legal aspects of this matter.
4 The manager asked me what my monthly salary was.
5 Jack spent the money he had won on a new car.
6 The accident was nobody's/not anyone's fault, in my opinion.
7 Sheila's parents strongly disapproved of her behaviour/the way she behaved at the party.
8 Roland could see nothing except/not see anything except the dark tower.
9 John is no longer scared of spiders.
10 'Yesterday the temperature rose significantly,' said the weatherman.

4

1	D	9	A
2	A	10	A
3	D	11	A
4	C	12	C
5	C	13	D
6	B	14	C
7	D	15	B
8	B		

5 Listening (page 59)

Tapescript

1 Well, what about Saturday – I don't mind afternoon or evening. Have you got anything? … 14K? How far back is it? … I see. So I'll get a good view of the stage from there, will I? O.K. I'll take it. Can I pay by credit card? I'll give you the number.

2 I'm sure this is the best one for you. It's made of a breathable, waterproof fabric so it will keep the rain out and you will stay dry and comfortable however much you sweat. It's got six pockets all with zips and it closes with a zip which is guaranteed never to get stuck, even in the coldest weather.

3 I went into the shop to buy some chocolate, but then I saw it on the shelf in the shop and it said on the cover 'Free inside – Everything you need to build your own aircraft' and I thought 'That's strange – you'd need a very big box for that.' Anyway, I bought it and when I opened it outside the shop I found that it was a paper aeroplane – a very advanced one which flew extremely well, I must say.

4 I first read about it on Monday. It was a fascinating story of a little boy of six and his sister who was four and how they had got lost in the mountains and survived for three weeks even though there were lots of dangerous animals about. There was more about it on Tuesday, as more details came out and it turned into a really big story. And then on Thursday it was on the television news.

5 When I got there I was surprised to find that the hall was empty – no one was there at all – and I was five minutes late, so I couldn't understand this at all. So I checked my invitation and, yes, it said 8 o'clock and this was the right place so I waited a bit but no one turned up. I couldn't understand it at all so I looked at the invitation again and it was only then that I realised that the meeting was the same time and day next week.

6 Is this for me? Is it really? Oh, you shouldn't have. There was no need, really. I didn't expect anything. It's very kind of you, it really is. I very much appreciate it. I wonder what it is. Can I open it now?

7 A: Could you tell us if, and when, these political reforms were actually carried out?

B: Now that's a very important question. In fact, all but one were eventually carried out but over a long period of time, but let us leave a detailed discussion of that until later in the course. In today's lecture, and also next week, I want to concentrate on why there was a demand for this kind of political change.

8 A: So where exactly is the problem?

B: Just here, where you see that little bit of rust.

A: Does it make a noise when you turn it?

B: Yes, especially when I'm going fast. It's been getting worse and sometimes it's very stiff and I have to press really hard to make it go. My legs get quite tired sometimes, especially around the ankles.

A: This part is very tight, isn't it? Let's try a bit of oil.

1	B	5	C
2	A	6	B
3	C	7	A
4	A	8	C

6 Listening (page 59)

Tapescript

Funnily enough one of my most beautiful places happened to be a village too, but it's in Britain and it's where I was brought up so probably, you know, it's covered with a haze of nostalgic memory. I was brought up in a small village called Fordwych which is outside Canterbury in Kent and it's a very very old village, all the buildings are old, and there's a very small town hall and a church and the church – we lived next to the church – and we lived in a very old house and some of the rafters in the roof were seven hundred years old or something. It's very very old, it had a great atmosphere. And my bedroom window looked out over the graveyard, and the graveyard was a lovely peaceful place and, as I say, that was right next to the house and then further on, if you walked past the church you walked down this road called the Drove, which was a long lane, and at the end of that was the river, the River Stour and that was always gorgeous and lovely and nobody was ever there except a few fishermen and as children we had that area to ourselves, and we could play there as much as we liked. And then if we wanted to, instead of going back along the Drove, we could go through the woods and somehow – maybe it's just memory – but the woods were always full of flowers in the spring, whereas these days when you look for bluebells or anemones and things you can't find them because people have uprooted them, but then, I think, we saw lots of primroses and bluebells and the woods smelt nice and the ground was dry and there were lots of leaves and pieces of bark and dust and it was untouched by humans. Obviously we were there but it wasn't spoilt in the way that these days woods have been organised and changed into picnic areas and things, and you could go up the hill through the woods and come down along a long winding lane which led back into the village. It was lovely.

1	village	6	woods
2	church	7	flowers
3	700 years	8	smell
4	graveyard	9	unspoilt
5	fishermen	10	picnics

unit 6 HOW THINGS WORK

Lead-in (page 60)

1 Check understanding of household words such as *central heating, lightbulb, switch, gas/electric fire, pipes, radiators, tank, plug*. The main aim is to discuss how the house depends on technology. The house needs electricity, for example, to light the house, to work the kitchen equipment, to work the computer/office, to work the TV and hi-fi. The TV needs the satellite dish to receive satellite television. The house needs gas to work the gas-fire in the lounge and perhaps the oven.

Some modern electrical appliances to bring to the students' attention are: *washing machine, dishwasher, kettle, computer, printer*. You can discuss what changes have taken place in the last 50 years and what changes might take place in the future.

Check that students realise that the picture shows a house which has a ground floor and a first floor.

2 1 b 2 d 3 a 4 h 5 e 6 c 7 f 8 g

3

1	make	10	engaged
2	receiver	11	line
3	call	12	switchboard operator
4	coins	13	put through
5	phonecard	14	extension number
6	collect call	15	hold
7	dial	16	connecting
8	buttons	17	hang up
9	ringing		

4

1	photograph	10	rewind
2	camera	11	developed
3	record	12	Prints
4	shutter	13	projector
5	automatic	14	image
6	flash	15	screen
7	slides	16	store
8	film	17	album
9	load	18	exposure

Reading: *The magic of the silver screen* (page 62)

A Find out how popular the cinema is among students, compared with other forms of entertainment.

Notes on the text

The Jazz Singer: strictly speaking this was the first feature film with synchronised sound. Short films had been made with sound before 1927.

B
1. very short films of one or two minutes
2. full-length films lasting at least two hours
3. sound which perfectly matches the movements of the actors' lips
4. someone plays the piano in the cinema as the film is shown
5. films in which the actors speak and can be heard by the audience
6. a written translation across the bottom of the screen
7. a translation of the actors' words spoken by another actor, forming a new soundtrack for the film
8. projecting a film onto a screen and filming scenes in front of it
9. showing on film things which could not happen in real life, usually done with models or computer simulation
10. stopping the camera, moving what is in front of it and starting the camera again – this is one way of making models move
11. screens which are much wider than usual
12. films which appear to have depth as well as width and height – this is usually achieved by wearing glasses with one lens green and the other red

C
1. The Lumière brothers showed a film in public for the first time in a cafe in Paris in 1895.
2. Audiences were terrified by a film by the Lumière brothers.
3. Early film makers enjoyed frightening the audience.
4. Back projection was used as early as 1913.
5. Feature films lasting two hours were being made by 1914.
6. *The Jazz Singer* was the first film to use synchronised sound.
7. The model used in *King Kong* was only

40 cm high.
8 Georges Méliès was the first to use the stop-action technique.
9 The model shark in *Jaws* had controls down one side.
10 Going to the cinema is less popular than it was in the first half of the century.

Grammar: *the passive form* (Grammar Notes **6.1**) (page 63)

1 All these sentences should be completed using passive forms. Revise the past participles of the verbs before doing the exercises.

A
1 he was murdered
2 are still being interviewed
3 hasn't been repaired
4 are made
5 has been stolen
6 was still being cleaned
7 has not been inhabited
8 is being done
9 will be sold/will have been sold
10 was told, had not yet been developed
11 had been forbidden
12 he had not been forgiven

B
1 Won't the painting be finished
2 Have the new procedures been explained
3 Was Mr Jones driven
4 are the offices cleaned
5 was Professor Sweet paid
6 Will the new swimming pool be opened
7 Weren't you shown
8 How many times has the grass been cut
9 were lost
10 will be watched by/is being watched by/is going to be watched by

C
1 will not be returned
2 may be offered
3 might be beaten
4 must have been stolen
5 should have been told
6 Does it have to be cooked
7 could have been forged
8 ought not to be treated/have been treated
9 must have been given
10 does not need to be replaced

2 (Grammar Notes **6.2**) (page 64)

1 No, it is very easy. There are no restrictions on membership.
2 Yes, very. He is ready to do terrible things.
3 Yes, it is the same.
4 Yes, he does very little work.
5 Very few people knew.
6 It is necessary to give a present but it doesn't matter what it is.
7 Yes, I like Bach's music – all of it.
8 Yes, I can fly on Tuesday – it doesn't matter what time.

Listening: *Surviving Air Crashes* (page 64)

Tapescript

DEBORAH: Professor Brown, you believe that passengers could survive most air crashes?

PROFESSOR BROWN: Yes, most crashes take place at low altitudes, soon after take-off or just before landing. We can improve passengers' ability to survive these crashes. The human body is fragile but if we pack it properly, just as we pack eggs, we can enable people to survive the impact of the crash. The most important thing is to have a new type of seat-belt which restrains the upper body. At the moment many people are killed or injured when their head is thrown forward and hits the seat in front. A seat-belt like the sort used in cars would prevent this. Secondly, more room between seats would prevent people from hitting the seat in front. Thirdly, having backward-facing seats would help passengers to survive the initial impact because they would be pressed back into their seats instead of being thrown forwards. Backward-facing seats are always fitted in military transport aircraft but not in civilian passenger aircraft. That's ridiculous, in my opinion. And another thing, there should be special child seats to provide adequate protection for children.

DEBORAH: Apart from the initial impact, what other dangers are there?

PROFESSOR BROWN: If passengers survive the impact, the next danger is from fire and smoke. If smoke hoods were available, they would help passengers to escape from a smoke-filled aircraft.

DEBORAH: But haven't experiments shown that smoke hoods are ineffective?

PROFESSOR BROWN: Well, those experiments used artificial smoke, which is not poisonous. But the real smoke in a crash would contain gases such as carbon monoxide. It would be poisonous and cause passengers to be overcome by fumes and fall to the floor. Smoke hoods would be helpful in these circumstances. So I don't accept the results of the experiments.

DEBORAH: Haven't airlines already introduced extra safety measures?

PROFESSOR BROWN: Yes, they have installed low-level lighting and smoke alarms in toilets. They should do a lot more, in my opinion.

DEBORAH: And what about sprinkler systems?

PROFESSOR BROWN: We don't know yet if they will be effective. Things are still at an experimental stage. There are problems about carrying large amounts of water in an aircraft where there are lots of electrical circuits.

DEBORAH: But won't improved safety lead to higher air fares?

PROFESSOR BROWN: Yes, it will. If special child seats are fitted then parents will have to pay more. There may be no more reduced fares for children. If there are wider spaces between seats, there will be fewer seats and therefore fewer passengers. This will lead to higher fares.

DEBORAH: What can passengers do to protect themselves?

PROFESSOR BROWN: They should not drink alcohol. They should pay attention to the safety announcements. They should dress suitably. In particular, women should not wear high-heeled shoes. They should not take heavy hand luggage onto the aircraft because the overhead bins are not designed to carry heavy objects. In the event of a crash, objects burst out of the bins and fall on people's heads.

DEBORAH: Why are airlines unwilling to introduce these changes?

PROFESSOR BROWN: It's a competitive world. Safety costs money and doesn't sell tickets. Improvements will only come about if government regulations compel all airlines to introduce the same safety measures at the same time.

1 A seat-belt for the upper body, more room between seats, backward-facing seats, special child seats, smoke hoods.
2 Smoke alarms in toilets, low-level lighting.
3 Don't drink alcohol, pay attention to safety announcements, dress suitably (no high heels), no heavy hand luggage in overhead bins.

English in Use (page 64)

1 Must be, could be (Grammar Notes **6.3**)

A
1 must
2 must
3 could
4 must
5 could

B
6 He must be late.
7 It must be a fake.
8 They could be genuine.
9 He could be in any of them.
10 There must be someone at home.

2 Invent, discover, find

Make sure that students realise that they may have to change the form of the word.

1 invented
2 (have) discovered/found
3 discovering/finding
4 found
5 established
6 found out/discovered
7 founded
8 inventions

Reading: *Holiday in space* (page 65)

1 **A** Such a holiday would offer the experience of weightlessness and spectacular views, freedom from crowds, excitement and possibly adventure.

B 1 F 2 G 3 D 4 C 5 H 6 E 7 B

Reading: *Enter a new world* (page 66)

A Students are likely to have experience of computer games. In the future, computers are likely to become smaller and perhaps controlled in different ways, by voice for example.

B

1	manipulate	6	scared
2	sensation	7	inconvenience
3	enhanced	8	remotely
4	adjusts	9	used to
5	risk	10	prolonged

C 1 They wear a headset and a glove.
2 They see computer-generated images and hear sound effects.
3 For training pilots, for training surgeons, for helping people overcome irrational fears, for learning foreign languages, for dangerous industrial processes.
4 People can have exciting experiences such as being an astronaut, a fighter pilot or taking part in a motor race.
5 It is more realistic and offers a more intense experience.
6 He believes that people may be badly affected in a psychological way and that many of the effects of VR are unknown.
7 Students must answer this question according to their own opinions.

Talking Points (page 67)

Section 1

The top photograph shows two children playing with a computer game. The centre photograph is a flight simulator and is obviously related to work. The bottom photograph is in fact taken from a computer programme which explains the Einstein equation and is related to study.

Check that students know basic computer words such as *monitor, screen, disc, printer, keyboard.* After the group discussion, it is a good idea to ask students to report on their discussions and to build up lists of words and ideas on the board.

Listening: *Supermarket checkouts* (page 67)

Tapescript

When you leave the supermarket these days, the chances are that the cashier will check out your goods by passing them over a special electronic machine that provides information to a computer. In order for the system to work, manufacturers have to use bar codes on their products. Bar codes indicate what the product is, which country it comes from and who the manufacturer is. An organisation called the 'Article Numbering Association' decides what the codes will be, and at the moment there are two sets of standard numbers. The numbered codes on the goods sold in a shop are entered into the shop's central computer, as well as information about the product, such as exactly what it was, how much it cost, which store it was sold in and whether there was a special offer available.

At the checkout, the operator passes the bar codes across a scanner which directs a beam of light on the code. It is the width of the lines and the space between them that is reflected back along the beam as a pattern of light and dark. The scanner decodes the lines into the code number which goes to the main computer. This sends back details of the product and the price to the checkout, where the information is printed on a roll on the till and can be passed to the customer. The computer keeps a record of the time, date and method of payment.

So what are the advantages of this type of checkout? From the customer's point of view, it must be that there are shorter queues at the checkout, as well as a till receipt that provides details of what was bought and how much each item cost. For the retailer, it improves the control of stock in the shop. At the end of each day, the retailer knows exactly what has been sold and so what needs to be re-ordered. Scanners can also tell the retailer how well a new product is selling, so that information can be acted on immediately.

1 scanner
2 till receipt
3 retailer
4 bar code
5 computer
6 customer

Writing: *Describing a process* (page 68)

1 **A** 1 First
2 then
3 Once
4 by
5 For example
6 Next
7 before
8 finally

B 1 The instructions can be a numbered list or continuous prose. Useful phrases are: *don't forget, remember to, please make sure that, pay particular attention to.*

2 Useful phrases are: *adjust the weights, perform ten times, change position, move the lever, check the safety catch, check your pulse rate, leave the machine as you found it, keep your legs bent, keep your back straight, breathe out as you lift the weight.*

Some common exercise machines are: *exercise bicycle, rowing machine.* Free weights are *barbells, dumbbells.*

English in Use (page 69)

1 Too, enough (Grammar Notes **6.4**)

1 too small
2 enough tickets
3 hot enough
4 enough experience
5 too heavy
6 too far away
7 enough
8 too sick to travel

2 **A** Rise, raise, arise

rise: is an intransitive verb meaning to go or travel upwards.
raise: is a transitive verb meaning something which is moved up.
arise: is an intransitive verb meaning something which comes to your attention or comes about.

B 1 rose
2 raise
3 risen
4 raise
5 arisen
6 arisen
7 raise
8 risen

3 Phrasal verbs

This exercise can be done as a speaking exercise in pairs. These answers are examples only. Provided that the phrasal verb is used, different sentences can be formed. For example, 3 could be 'Yes, I don't want to carry on.'

1 He made off with it.
2 No, it has been called off.
3 No, let's carry on.
4 No, I don't think it will catch on.
5 I came across it in a charity shop.
6 The researchers ran out of money.
7 We'll just have to do without.
8 No, he hasn't got over his illness yet.

4 Word-formation

1 suspicious
2 careful
3 poisonous
4 helpful
5 ambitious
6 disastrous
7 courageous

unit 7 THE FAMILY

Lead-in (page 70)

1 The photograph is in fact of six generations of the same family together. Students should be encouraged to describe the family relationships in the photograph, and to demonstrate knowledge of words such as *mother, father, child, grandfather, great-grandmother, niece, nephew, cousin, aunt, uncle, related to, related by marriage.*

They can move on to discuss the roles each family member plays. e.g. grandparents looking after young children while the parents go out to work and issues such as having step-brothers and sisters, being adopted, being fostered, living in a children's home.

2
1 bachelor
2 elderly
3 Adoption
4 step-brothers
5 orphans
6 in-laws
7 great-grandparents
8 toddler
9 single
10 widow

3
1 close
2 engaged
3 fiancé
4 introduced
5 wedding
6 give up
7 home
8 depended
9 pregnant
10 running
11 bringing up
12 support
13 intention
14 career
15 plan
16 nanny
17 benefit
18 independent
19 work out
20 split up

Reading: *Anita Roddick* (page 72)

A Students should discuss the questions in pairs or groups of three and give their views on the importance of family life and relationships. They should deal with the advantages of family life (help and support), as well as the disadvantages (restrictions, obligations). They should discuss the roles of different family members, and what is expected from each member of the family.

Notes on the text

Anita Roddick is the founder of the extremely successful chain of shops, *The Body Shop.*They sell toiletries and cosmetics which are not tested on animals.

terraced house: a house joined to others in a continuous row, referred to here to indicate the family's modest background

our café: Anita's mother made her living by running a café

B
1 nanny
2 home village
3 confidence
4 maddening
5 work ethic
6 hideous

C 1 D 2 C 3 A 4 D 5 D

Grammar: *present perfect* (Grammar Notes **7.1**) (page 73)

A
a My finger is bleeding.
b In the cave.
c No.
d Yes.
e Yes.

1 False.
2 False.
3 False.
} please refer to the Grammar Notes **7.1** (page 228)

B
1 We have already sold two hundred tickets and there is still a month to go before the concert.
2 I have never visited New York.
3 Have you ever thought of learning to fly?
4 I have just received my exam result.
5 Janet hasn't finished yet with the camera. *or* Janet hasn't finished with the camera yet.

C Students should first pick out the two sentences (nos. 6 and 7) where it is impossible to use the present perfect because of the past time reference e.g. *in 1990, three days ago*. There are many possible answers here. The following are provided as suggestions only.

1 I have visited fifteen countries so far.
2 The two countries have been at war for ten years.
3 I haven't seen Samantha since I left school.
4 Helen's worked for the Inland Revenue since 1990.
5 I've loved this piece of music for as long as I can remember.
6 This example cannot be completed with a verb in the present perfect.
The Director resigned in 1990.
7 This example cannot be completed with a verb in the present perfect.
George left the country three days ago.

D These are suggestions. There are many other possible answers.

1 No, he's just gone to the supermarket.
2 Yes, he's been kept fully informed.
3 No, the children have eaten it all.
4 No, they've moved.
5 No, I haven't read it.

E
1 has entered, has never won
2 have continued, started
3 didn't come, took
4 have you been, expected
5 first went, have been back
6 have waited, has arrived

Listening: *A family photo* (page 74)

Tapescript

INTERVIEWER: Right, can you describe the photograph you're looking at?

KATHERINE: Well actually it's quite an … an important photograph for me because it's a picture of my parents getting married and erm … I suppose it's quite a few years ago now. Erm, and it's a black and white photograph so it's not very … erm … well it's difficult, well I can't talk about the colours but erm … it's quite a nice photograph. They're standing outside the church. They must've just been married. Erm they look terribly old-fashioned now, actually. Erm … my mother's got a suit on 'cause it was just after the war … erm people didn't have very much money then, everybody was broke, erm … it's quite a smart tailored suit and high-heeled shoes and poli … very polished shoes and a big bouquet of roses. She's also wearing a brooch and it's very sad, she's dead now and that brooch my father gave to me as a, as a present, and not many years ago I was walking along the street and I was wearing this brooch and it must've fallen off … and it's … I was very upset about it at the time because it's the, the brooch she had on in this photograph. And I put an advertisement in the newspaper and I, I did everything that you can do when you've lost a brooch, put notices in the newsagent's, but I never got it back, and it wasn't really valuable but it was sentimentally important, it was of sentimental value. Erm, my father's wearing a carnation, and erm he looks terribly old-fashioned with a moustache and short back-and-sides, that sort of look, erm a suit and a waistcoat and erm white gloves which probably people wouldn't wear now and erm, that's all really. They both look very happy and I suppose they're just off to the reception.

1 It's a wedding photograph of the speaker's mother and father.
2 No.
3 Outside the church.
4 A (smart tailored) suit, high-heeled shoes and a brooch.
5 A suit, a waistcoat, white gloves and a carnation.
6 A bouquet of roses.
7 A brooch.
8 Her father gave it to her after her mother died.
9 It fell off when she was wearing it.
10 Very upset.
11 She put an advertisement in the paper and in the newsagent's.
12 It was not valuable in terms of money but it had great sentimental value for her.

English in Use (page 74)

1 Prepositions

1 to, out
2 in, with
3 to
4 to
5 of
6 by
7 off, to
8 up
9 of
10 to

2
1 ✓
2 all
3 ✓
4 ✓
5 out
6 much
7 with
8 are
9 for
10 of
11 to
12 up
13 a
14 ✓
15 that

Reading: *Weddings* (page 75)

A Students should discuss the legal aspects of a wedding as well as the social conventions.

Notes on the text

The Church of England: people married in religious ceremonies recognised by law do not have to have an additional ceremony in a registry office

an Elizabethan manor: a country house dating from the sixteenth century

a receiving line: the married couple and their relatives stand in a line and talk to each of their guests in turn as they walk past

Glasgow: a major city in Scotland

an arranged marriage: the traditional arrangement in certain cultures of the parents choosing the marriage partner for their children

henna: a reddish-brown dye

a kilted piper: a piper is a man who plays the traditional Scottish instrument, the bagpipes; he wears a kilt, the traditional tartan skirt worn by Scottish men (see Unit 1, Listening)

tuxedo: an American style dress suit

a complimentary limo: a limousine provided free for the occasion

Lulworth Cove: a beautiful part of the coast in Dorset, in the south of England

a brilliant place: a wonderful place (a colloquial and very common term meaning very good)

a traditional/big do: a traditional/big party

a Cajun band: a band performing music typical of the Cajuns, people of French-Canadian origin who settled in Louisiana, USA

B
1 C
2 B
3 A, C
4 D
5 A, B, D
6 C
7 A, B, D
8 A, B

Reading: *I'm serving a sentence too* (page 76)

A Students should be encouraged to discuss the difficulties faced by families where one of the parents has been sent to gaol and the family is left alone to manage by themselves. They should consider the social consequences (the attitude of neighbours/friends) as well as the personal consequences (loneliness, lack of money, family tensions).

Notes on the text

a daddy's girl: a girl who is very fond of her father and has a special relationship with him

B 1 B 2 A 3 C 4 C 5 B 6 C

C
1 No, she didn't.
2 She says he was desperate as a result of being out of work.
3 No, she doesn't.
4 To provide some protection and make her feel more secure.
5 Twice a month.
6 Very bad. She is in debt.
7 They are surprised Sakina stays with him.
8 She won't stay with him then.
9 Yes, because both of them will have to adjust to changes in their relationship.

Talking Points (page 77)

Section 1

The photograph on the left shows two people, probably in their sixties, in a smallish garden, doing the gardening. The man is weeding or digging and the woman is watering a tree. They are obviously fit and active. The photograph on the right shows an elderly couple, probably in their seventies, relaxing in chairs around a table. It looks as if the man is reading a newspaper and the woman is reading a book. They look older and less mobile than the people in the photograph on the left.

Section 2

The students should cover the topic of dealing with old people on a personal level, in terms of how it affects individual families and the relationships within them, and the general social problem of an aging population. They should discuss the difficulties old people themselves face (health, loss of mobility, bereavement, financial problems, coping) as well as the general problem of housing and caring for them.

Listening: Childhood memories (page 78)

Tapescript

Well, this photograph that I've got in front of me is a very old one. It's in black and white, of course, because they didn't have colour then, or to be more accurate it's a brownish sort of colour. It was taken in 1916 and it shows my grandfather who was in fact sixteen when it was taken. And in this photo he's wearing army uniform with a cap and a big belt and so on. You may be wondering why he was in the army when he was only sixteen. Well, the reason is that he told the recruiting officers that he was eighteen, which was the minimum age for joining the army, and they believed him, or wanted to believe him. Anyway, they didn't check and he joined up. I think this photo was taken soon after he joined and before he was sent to France because he looks very fresh and innocent. In fact, he left the army before he had reached the minimum age for joining because he was wounded and sent back to England. I know that for the rest of his life he wasn't in good health, partly because of this wound and he died at the fairly young age of sixty. I was only seven when he died so I never really had a chance to talk to him about his life. I remember him very well though, even now. In fact one of my strongest memories, and earliest memories, is of a time when he was a bit angry with me. I must have been about four at the time and my grandfather, who was very fond of gardening, as I am too, had grown some onions and let them go to seed so that he could use the seeds to grow more onions next year. So I saw these onions, which had big round heads full of seeds and were as tall as me and I took a stick and I knocked all the heads off the onions and the air was full of all these onion seeds, which are very light, so the wind blew them all over the place and when my grandfather discovered what I'd done I said something like 'Pretty flowers, grandad,' and he said 'I'll give you "pretty flowers" – they're my prize onions.'

1 1916.
2 Army uniform.
3 Sixteen.
4 He was too young to be in the army but he had lied about his age.
5 He was wounded during the war.
6 He regrets that he was unable to talk to his grandfather about his life because his grandfather died when he was seven.
7 He likes gardening.
8 He remembers his grandfather being displeased when he knocked the seedheads off his onions.

Writing: *A letter of advice* (page 78)

There is room for flexibility in the answer as there is no single 'correct' response. Students should demonstrate that they have considered all the possibilities and provide a balanced answer.

English in Use (page 79)

1 **A** 1 a 2 c 3 b

B The first question refers to a person's appearance. The second refers to both character and appearance, while the third is about the things that person likes.

C
1 What is Alice like?
2 What do Anna and Helen look like?
3 What does Kevin like?
4 What is the house like?
5 Do you like lettuce?
6 What does Patrick look like? *or* What is Patrick like?
7 What is John like?
8 As a student, what is Shirley like?
9 What will the weather be like tomorrow?
10 Did you like the film?

2 Phrasal verbs

1 took up
2 took out
3 took away
4 take off
5 takes after
6 take it out on
7 take … in
8 takes on
9 take off
10 take … in

3 Word-formation

1 physicist
2 trainee
3 historian
4 pianist
5 Politicians
6 employee
7 psychologist
8 magician
9 scientists
10 beautician

unit 8 GOOD COMPANIONS

Lead-in (page 80)

1 The photographs introduce the two themes of his unit: people's relationships with each other as riends, colleagues, fellow-students, and people's elationships with animals.

2
1 colleagues
2 outsiders
3 acquaintances
4 schoolfriends
5 penpals

3
1 team
2 crew
3 staff
4 crowd
5 mob
6 gang
7 audience
8 spectators
9 fans
10 congregation

4
1 criticised
2 congratulate
3 motivate
4 encouraged
5 praised
6 support
7 trust
8 betrayed
9 make, keep
10 boosted

Reading: *Dolphin's mystery powers cure slim-mad Jemima* (page 82)

A Probably people like dolphins because they are ntelligent, playful, easily trained, obviously ommunicate with each other, are not dangerous, lo tricks and seem to like humans.

Animals may make people feel good because they re uncritical, very loyal and dependable and offer a ot of companionship.

B
1 undergo
2 curing
3 tamed
4 suffering
5 weight
6 depressed
7 pioneer
8 plunge
9 haul
10 exhilaration
11 stroking
12 reassured

C In the sea off the north coast of Britain, Jemima Biggs, 25, has been swimming with Freddie, a 4-metre long, 275-kilogram wild dolphin. Swimming with this dolphin is helping Jemima to overcome anorexia nervosa, a disease which causes her to lose weight – she doesn't know how much she weighs but it is probably about 41 kilograms. She is making progress now and she can eat with other people but she still doesn't weigh herself. Jemima is a postgraduate student at Exeter University and travels a long distance every weekend to swim with Freddie. The treatment is supervised by Dr Horace Dobbs, who was contacted by Jemima after her mother saw a television programme about his work. Jemima has had six or seven sessions with Freddie and plays with him for about ten minutes and touches him a lot. Dr Dobbs has made a tape of music and dolphin sounds to help people who are unable to come to visit.

Grammar: *present perfect (simple and continuous)* (Grammar Notes **8.1**) (page 83)

A A variety of answers are possible. These are examples only.

1 I've been running.
2 I've been painting.
3 I've been working very hard.
4 I've been walking in the woods.
5 I've been baking bread.
6 I've been swimming.

B Again, many answers are possible.

1 have you been waiting
2 have you been playing
3 have you been studying
4 have you been working
5 have you been taking

6 Have you been suffering
7 Have you been trying

C
a Once, by accident.
b Several times, continuously, which is unlikely.
c This sentence is fine.
d This sentence is impossible.
e This sentence is fine.
f This sentence is unlikely, unless it is meant metaphorically meaning that the husband has suffered a slow and painful death.

D
1 have found
2 have been searching, have not found
3 have been losing
4 have lost
5 has fallen
6 has stolen
7 have accidentally torn
8 has been eating
9 have been pecking
10 have been analysing, have found

E
1 took, have failed
2 composed, has composed
3 bought, haven't built
4 moved, have lived
5 saw, have seen
6 didn't have, have had
7 hasn't flown, got
8 haven't seen, saw
9 was, hasn't been
10 met, have been

Listening: *Pets as therapy* (page 84)

Make sure that students realise that they can use *one* or *two* words but not more.

Tapescript

In the 1970s a group of American doctors carried out a special study of patients who had had heart operations. They wanted to discover why some patients lived much longer after the operation than others did. They compared patients according to age, sex, race and social status but none of these factors seemed to make a difference to how long they survived. Astonishingly, they discovered that 6% of people who owned a pet died within one year of the operation but 28% of those who did not own a pet died within one year. Owning or not owning a pet was the most significant factor in determining how long patients survived. It seems that the companionship provided by a pet and the responsibility of looking after one gave people a reason for living. In the last twenty years many doctors have encouraged people who are seriously ill to take an interest in animals in the belief that it will speed up their recovery.

Animals have also been used as a form of therapy with people who are physically or mentally handicapped. One of the most successful schemes has involved the teaching of horse-riding to handicapped children. These children gain a tremendous amount of confidence when they are able to control a large animal. As they learn to ride, they also improve their own physical co-ordination. Animals have also been used successfully with people who are suffering from depression.

As well as improving the way that people feel about themselves and the world, animals can also perform very practical tasks. We are all familiar with guide dogs used by blind people but in recent years Capuchin monkeys, one of the most intelligent types of monkey, have been trained to help disabled people by fetching things for them, switching lights on and off and so on. The monkeys are carefully trained but wear a strap round their bodies so that, if they misbehave, their disabled owner can give them a mild electric shock. In this case the benefits to the owner are practical rather than psychological.

1 heart operations
2 6%
3 28%
4 recovery
5 (horse) riding
6 (Capuchin) monkeys
7 electric shocks

English in Use: *Definite article* (Grammar Notes **8.2**) (page 84)

The ten correct sentences are: 3, 4, 7, 8, 9, 10, 11, 14, 19, 20. Correct version of incorrect sentences:

D 1 had won
2 looked
3 found, had escaped
4 appeared
5 had left
6 had not been stolen

Listening: *An accident on a motorbike* (page 118)

Tapescript

INTERVIEWER: So have you ever had any accidents?

REBECCA: Well the worst accident that I've had by far was a motorbike accident. And er, I was riding my motorbike to work one day and er the car in front of me did an emergency stop and although I wasn't riding that close to the back of the car, erm, I was only on a smallish, lightweight motorbike and I just couldn't stop that quickly, and er, I put my brakes on, but erm I went into the back of the car and the next thing I knew I was flying through the air and er, unfortunately I landed on the back lights of a parked car nearby. And because the weather was very fine that day and er, I was only wearing a skirt, in other words er, I'd got bare legs, and er, the next thing I knew, I was sitting on the pavement and when I opened my eyes, er, my er, right leg was full of pieces of glass and plastic from the, the back lights of this car that I'd landed on, and er, all sorts of things that should have been inside my leg were kind of … hanging out. And er, well, it wasn't a very pretty sight. Erm, fortunately it happened opposite a garage and they heard the sound of this crash, and er immediately ran out to see what had happened and then ran back and phoned for an ambulance and within, oh, something like ten minutes I was er I was in the hospital, er being treated, and er … er in the end it wasn't too bad. I was in hospital for about ten days and I had dozens and dozens of stitches in my leg, er but I couldn't walk for about two months.

1	False	3	False
2	False	4	True
5	True	9	False
6	True	10	True
7	False	11	False
8	False	12	True

English in Use (page 118)

1 wound, injure, injury, damage (Grammar Notes **11.2**)

1	wounded	6	injuries
2	damage	7	damaged
3	injured	8	wounded
4	wound	9	damaged
5	damage	10	wound

2 heal, cure, treat (Grammar Notes **11.3**)

1	cure, treat	6	treat
2	cure	7	heal
3	healed	8	cure, treat
4	heal	9	cured
5	cure	10	healing

3

1	from	5	from
2	in	6	for
3	on	7	with
4	to	8	from/of

Reading: *The lifelong penalty facing football-crazy youngsters* (page 119)

A Students should discuss in small groups the sports and exercise they participate in, and then how they feel about the injuries common to their sport.

Notes on the text

The Football Association (The FA): the controlling body of the game in Great Britain

B 1 B 2 D 3 C 4 C 5 C

Reading: *Survivors* (page 120)

A Students should talk about what they would consider a bad experience, such as *failing exams, having to give up schooling, having to move from an area where they were happy, an accident, being made redundant*, and then talk about what makes some people able to cope better than others. They could mention *perseverance*, *guts*, *confidence*, *not giving up*.

Notes on the text

out of the blue: suddenly

bloated: swollen

temping: temporary

B Text 1

Medical expressions which occur in the text:

1. *a liver transplant*: an operation to give somebody another person's liver
2. *her heart stopped beating*: her heart stopped working
3. *I started to vomit*: I started to be sick
4. *I was putting on a lot of weight*: I became heavier
5. *I felt so bloated*: I felt so swollen
6. *I was retaining loads of fluid*: I was keeping in all the water in my body
7. *I went into a coma*: I lost consciousness for a very long time
8. *my liver had failed*: my liver had stopped working
9. *I started to bleed internally*: I started to bleed inside
10. *the doctors managed to revive me*: the doctors succeeded in bringing me back to life
11. *brain-damaged*: mentally or physically handicapped
12. *the oxygen supply to my brain had been cut off*: oxygen was not reaching my brain

Text 2

Negative words:

1. devastated
2. I couldn't speak
3. I felt I was utterly worthless
4. just cast aside
5. I got so depressed
6. I just broke down and cried

Rachel: 1, 4, 5, 6, 7

Karen: 2, 3, 8, 9, 10

Talking Points (page 121)

Section 1

Students should describe the scenes in the photos, outline what has happened and suggest ways of dealing with the situation.

In the photograph on the left the car has a flat tyre/puncture. One way of dealing with this situation could be to replace the wheel with the spare wheel and take the punctured tyre to the garage to be mended. The photograph on the right shows a cat, obviously frightened, stuck in a tree. In this situation you could try and rescue the cat yourself (if you have a long enough ladder), or phone the fire-brigade.

Section 2

Students should explore the possibilities of handling the situations. Some suggestions for giving advice would be:

1. Why don't you send him/her a belated birthday card?
2. It would be a good idea to offer to buy him/her a new book.
3. I suggest you put on some 'after sun' and stay out of the sun for a couple of days.
4. What about taking it to the local bike shop to be repaired?
5. Have you thought of putting an advert in the local newsagent's?

Listening: *Narrow escapes* (page 122)

Tapescript

INTERVIEWER: So can you tell me about the narrow escape that you've had?

KATHERINE: Well it was when I was a very small child erm, and it's very odd because I still remember it very vividly even though I was only about four or five. But it must be one of my earliest memories, erm we'd all gone to my uncle's for a family gathering and we were, we were all sitting round and talking and we were eating and things and I was sitting near the fire, and it was a big open fire, and I was sort of laughing. And then I leant back, and erm suddenly my hair caught fire and there was this awful smell of singed hair everywhere and my uncle sort of picked me up and grabbed me and started banging me about the head and everybody got a wet towel, and I had all this singed, black hair, and er it gave me ever such a shock. And I suppose that is quite a narrow escape really!

DAVID: It's … this incident happened erm in winter, erm we have an open fire in winter and erm it was when my, my eldest son had reached an age where he could actually clear out the ashes and put them outside. I think it was the first time he'd done it. He'd cleared out the ashes erm, and put them straight into a plastic dustbin which was in a shed outside. I was due to go out that evening and er at the very last moment erm, my friend rang to cancel. It was just going out for … to the theatre or to the cinema, I can't remember quite which, and I'd got back from work and I just happened to be preparing a meal in the kitchen and suddenly if I … if I hadn't been in the kitchen at that time, or had been out, I wouldn't have seen the flames outside the back door as the shed was absolutely destroyed by the, by the fire which developed inside the plastic bag, inside the dustbin, burnt the shed down and burnt the outside of the house and if nobody had been in the house the whole house would have been burned down.

1 David
2 Katherine and David
3 Katherine
4 David
5 Katherine
6 David
7 Katherine and David
8 Katherine
9 Katherine and David
10 David

Writing: *A letter to a company* (page 122)

Students should use the phrases provided to help them in their letter writing. The sentences provided come from:

1 Final paragraph
2 Opening/Introductory paragraph
3 Ending
4 Second paragraph

English in Use: (page 121)

1 Phrasal verbs

1	stand for	6	stand up for
2	stood up	7	stand down
3	standing by	8	stand up
4	stood out	9	stood aside
5	stand for	10	stand for

2 Word-formation

1	deliveries	6	paralysis
2	signature	7	pressure
3	closure	8	injuries
4	expiry	9	emphasis
5	prosperity	10	seizure

unit 12 WEATHER AND CLIMATE

Lead-in (page 124)

1 In the top photograph a man is looking at his crops which have burnt and died because of a drought. The ground looks hard and cracked. It unfortunately also looks likely that there will be a famine in the area. In the bottom photograph a coastline is being battered by a tornado. Storm damage is obvious: trees have been blown down and litter the beach. There is a strong possibility of floods because of an angry-looking sea and a rising tide.

Elicit from the students vocabulary concerning the extremes of weather such as *flooding*, *storms*, *hurricanes*, *tornados*, *droughts* and the consequences such as *trees being blown down*, *roofs being lifted off*, *people getting trapped*, *damage to property*, *making insurance claims*, *loss of livelihood and starvation*.

2

1	heatwave	6	hail storm
2	drought	7	gale
3	avalanche	8	lightning
4	fog	9	climate
5	breeze	10	mist

3

1	erode	6	swept
2	frostbite	7	drenched
3	irrigate	8	sunstroke
4	famine	9	cut off
5	flooded	10	evacuate

Reading: *Storms Sweep Britain: 16 die* (page 126)

A Check that students understand the difference between 'worse' and 'worst'. Elicit from students problems caused by bad weather such as *damage to buildings*, *disruption of transport services*, *damage to crops*, *interruption of building work*, *cancellation of sports fixtures*.

Make sure that students understand what *tides* are and what effect they have, especially if they are from countries where there are no tides. Remember that in Britain the difference between high tide and low tide is very large.

B
1 16 people were killed
2 2 metres – the depth of the floods
3 2,000 people were evacuated
4 50 people were taken to hospital
5 8 motorists were killed
6 150 kph – the speed of the winds

C Note that in these phrasal verbs both the main verb and the particles have predictable meanings.

to sweep across: movement of wind across the country

to sweep through: movement of flood water through the streets

to blow onto: movement of the wind making something fly through the air and hit someone or something

to blow down: movement of the wind causing things to fall

to blow off: movement of the wind causing something to be separated from something else

to blow aground: movement of the wind causing ships to get stuck on the beach or in mud

D 1 B 2 A 3 B

Grammar: *conditionals* (Grammar Notes 12.1) (page 127)

A I didn't know about the danger.
I didn't warn you.

Yes, you told me.
No, I didn't know.

Yes, he saw the cyclist.
No there wasn't an accident.

B 1 c 2 a 3 b 4 e 5 d

C These are example answers. Others are possible.
1 … we wouldn't have drunk it.
2 … he would have gone by car.
3 … she would probably have become ill.
4 … he hadn't driven through a red light.
5 … the helicopter hadn't lifted them off the ship.

D These are example sentences. Others are possible.

If he had heard his alarm, he wouldn't have missed his train.

If he had put less in his suitcase, he would not have had to pay a charge.

If he hadn't been in a hurry, he wouldn't have gone to the wrong gate.

If he hadn't eaten the food on the plane, he wouldn't have felt sick.

If he had put on some suntan lotion, he wouldn't have got sunburnt.

If he had locked his room, his watch wouldn't have been stolen.

E These are example answers. Others are possible.

1 If we had known that the museum was free yesterday, we would have gone then.
2 If you change your flight to Friday, I can give you an earlier flight.
3 If we had seen the note our friends had left for us, we would have known where they had gone.
4 If we could afford to replace the central heating, our house would be warmer.
5 If we had seen the signpost, we would have taken the right turning.

Listening: *Weather forecasts* (page 128)

Tapescript

1 There will be some early morning mist which will soon be dispersed by the heat of the sun. The morning and early afternoon will be sunny and warm but by late afternoon it will cloud over and there will be showers by evening.

2 The morning will start off grey and overcast with a little sun in the middle of the day but becoming very cloudy again later. Showers will be followed by heavier rain and strong winds. There could be gales during the night so you are advised to put your car in the garage and secure any loose objects, such as tables and chairs, which might be in your garden.

3 The day will be bright, clear and sunny but rather cold. Temperatures will remain at or near freezing. Snow may fall in the evening and there will be a sharp frost tonight.

4 Temperatures will remain high for the time of year but strong winds will make it seem cold. The winds will die down towards the evening but heavy rain will continue through the night.

1 B 2 C 3 D 4 A

English in Use (page 128)

1 Bath, bathe, sunbathe (Grammar Notes 12.2)

1 bath
2 bath
3 sunbathe
4 bathe
5 bath
6 bathe
7 sunbathe
8 Bathe
9 bathe
10 Sunbathing

2 Short forms (Grammar Notes 12.3)

1 does
2 won't
3 didn't
4 don't/haven't
5 have
6 didn't
7 should
8 can't
9 hadn't
10 wouldn't

Reading: *Is winter a disease?* (page 129)

B
1 feeling depressed in winter
2 signs of illness
3 people who repeatedly get ill
4 life became too difficult for her
5 sleepy
6 collapsed, with arms and legs hanging loosely
7 very slow
8 completely without hope
9 sleep in winter
10 very active

C
1 It stands for Seasonal Affective Disorder – feeling depressed in winter.
2 In northern countries about 20% of people have SAD to some degree and 5% suffer from it seriously.
3 She slept longer than usual, felt drowsy, ate more, spent hours in an armchair in front of the TV, often burst into tears, put on weight and felt sluggish.
4 She could not face going to work in the dark and coming home in the dark.
5 Dr MacRae is the expert on SAD and knows how to cure it.
6 He put a special lightbox in Janet's home.
7 It is caused by lack of light.
8 They become very energetic in spring – they talk a lot and cannot sleep or sit still.

Reading: *Water, water everywhere – or is there?* (page 130)

A Water can be obtained from taps in the house, from pumps outside the house, from wells, from rivers and water-holes, from tanks that catch rainwater, from reservoirs that store water and from bottles bought in shops. Water is usually paid for either by a flat-rate charge or according to how much you use, recorded by a meter. We could be more economical in our use of water by using only what we need, by having showers instead of baths, not watering the garden, not washing the car, not leaving the tap running when we wash our teeth etc.

Notes on the text

survival without food: Angus Barbieri survived without food for 382 days in Dundee Hospital from June 1965 to July 1966. He lived on tea, coffee and vitamins. His weight went down from 214 kg to 80 kg.

B 1 B 2 A 3 C 4 H 5 F 6 G 7 D

Talking Points (page 131)

Section 1

Students must work in pairs and find clues in **List A** which go with **List B**. For example, the reference to 'rain' in 1 is clearly linked to getting 'soaked to the skin' in b.

1 b 2 e 3 g 4 a 5 c 6 h 7 f 8 d 9 i

Section 2

There are two current theories on climate change: the first states that it is likely to get hotter in the next fifty years because of the greenhouse effect. That is, the CFCs and carbon gases will attack the ozone layer and create holes in it. These holes will let in unfiltered sun's rays which will heat up the atmosphere, melt the icebergs and increase the sea level; the second theory states that the damage to the ozone layer will in effect let the warm carbon gases escape thereby leading to a cooler climate. Holes in the ozone layer will also mean that the sun's rays will bounce off the earth and return to the outer atmosphere and lead to a second Ice Age.

Section 3

Encourage students to discuss whether or not they agree with the stereotypical view that living in a cold climate makes people 'cold'.

Listening: *Freak weather* (page 132)

Tapescript

INTERVIEWER: Professor Marsh, you are an expert on freak weather conditions and in fact you have just written a book full of amazing stories of very unusual weather. What first attracted you to this field of study?

PROFESSOR MARSH: Well, Nick, people used to explain unusual weather by saying it was caused by magic or by the gods but of course there are scientific explanations for these things although I have to admit that there are a few things that we haven't found the answers to yet but I enjoy trying to find rational scientific explanations for phenomena which at first sight seem strange and mysterious.

INTERVIEWER: Can you give an example?

PROFESSOR MARSH: Well, you probably heard stories about 'raining blood' (*INTERVIEWER:* Yes.) There are lots of such stories in ancient and medieval history and people used to think that it was a sign that something terrible was going to happen but we know now that these showers of blood happen when a wind picks up red sand from a desert region and carries it hundreds of miles to a place where red sand is unknown. When it rains, the sand dyes the raindrops red and people think it is blood.

INTERVIEWER: And is that the explanation for the showers of fish and frogs?

PROFESSOR MARSH: Exactly. The wind has picked them up from the sea or a lake and dropped them somewhere else.

INTERVIEWER: But is the wind strong enough to do such things?

PROFESSOR MARSH: Oh yes, definitely. In fact, in 1880 in the United States a tornado picked up a house and carried it 19 kilometres through the air and then dropped it – still in one piece – I don't think anyone was at home at the time – and there is another incident, it happened in China in 1986, of twelve children being picked up by a tornado and carried through the air for 20 kilometres and they were completely unharmed by this experience. (*INTERVIEWER*: Amazing.) Both these stories are absolutely true. There's another story, which I haven't been able to verify, of a motorist who was driving along – it was somewhere in the mid-west of the United States – when his car was struck by a tornado – it was summer and he was driving an open car – and he crashed but he wasn't injured and when he turned round he saw someone in the back of the car who he didn't know and who hadn't been there before. Apparently, the tornado had picked up this person somewhere else and dropped him there.

INTERVIEWER: You said that there were some things you couldn't explain?

PROFESSOR MARSH: Yes, well not yet, anyway. There is a very strange phenomenon known as 'crop circles' where round shapes, they're usually round, but sometimes other shapes, appear in fields of wheat or other growing crops. They are best seen from the air and some people think that they are caused by flying saucers or fairies or whatever.

INTERVIEWER: But you don't believe that?

PROFESSOR MARSH: No, I certainly don't. I'm a scientist! They are probably caused by some sort of wind, a sort of mini tornado, but so far no one has actually seen one happening so they are still a bit of a mystery.

A
1. She likes to find scientific explanations for mysterious happenings.
2. 'Raining blood' which is caused by red sand picked up by the wind and 'raining fish' which are also picked up by the wind.
3. She says that in 1880 a house was carried 19 kilometres by a tornado in the United States and that in 1986 in China twelve children were carried 20 kilometres in a tornado. She says that a motorist who had crashed his car found a stranger in the back seat of the car, apparently dropped there by a tornado.
4. She has not verified the story about the motorist.
5. She cannot explain 'crop circles'.
6. Some people think that crop circles are caused by flying saucers or fairies but she thinks that they are caused by wind.

Writing: *A summary* (page 132)

The article need not use all the information available. Students should be selective.

English in Use (page 133)

1 What, which (Grammar Notes **12.4**)

1	what	6	which
2	which	7	what
3	which	8	what
4	what	9	which
5	which	10	what

2 Phrasal verbs

1	cut	5	keep
2	see	6	broken
3	blasted	7	run
4	get	8	give

3 Word-formation

1	postponement	3	storage
2	reaction	4	improvement

5 election
6 enlargement
7 wreckage
8 predictions
9 passage
10 protection

unit 13 HEROES AND HEROINES?

Lead-in (page 134)

1 The two figures, Napoleon and Columbus, have been chosen because of the various ways, both positive and negative, in which their actions can be viewed. Students should be able to consider different aspects of each person's behaviour.

Napoleon (1769–1821): educated Military Academy Brienne; married Josephine Beauharnais 1796; established a military dictatorship in France in 1799; assumed the title of Emperor of France in 1804; made a lasting impact on the country through the Code Napoleon; forced to abdicate in 1814; returned to France but was defeated at the Battle of Waterloo by a coalition of forces led by the Duke of Wellington; banished to the island of St Helena.

Columbus (1451–1506): born Genoa Italy 1451; went to sea at the age of 14; had plans to reach India by sailing West; plans approved and backed by Ferdinand and Isabella of Spain; set sail in 1492 and in fact reached the Bahamas, Cuba and Latin America.

2
1 star
2 legend
3 heroism
4 criticism
5 respect
6 defeat
7 failure
8 hero-worship
9 success
10 coward

3
1 achievements
2 in the public eye
3 well-known
4 autograph
5 on show
6 commented
7 privacy
8 dodge
9 fans
10 celebrities
11 private life
12 intruders
13 interviews
14 publicity

Reading: *Grace Darling* (page 136)

A Students here should limit their discussion to heroism and bravery, and to the effect of this on people's lifestyle. Areas to touch upon could be honouring or commemorating bravery publicly by giving the person a title or a medal.

B 1 C 2 C 3 B 4 C 5 B 6 C 7 B

C
1 Grace's father was a lighthouse keeper.
2 Her childhood was difficult because she had a very strict religious upbringing.
3 She had a life of drudgery, spending her time cooking and cleaning.
4 They rescued only the five passengers who had managed to swim to the rocks.
5 Some journalists wrote about her without having met her.
6 Many stories were made up and not true.
7 Money was collected for her in recognition of her bravery.
8 Although she received many offers of marriage, Grace was not interested in them and turned them all down.
9 She found her life badly affected by becoming famous.
10 Grace's father could not understand the public reaction to his daughter.

Grammar: *revision of past tenses* (Grammar Notes **13.1**) (page 137)

A
1 The shouting took place first. She walked away when she heard the shout. No action was interrupted.
2 The woman was in the process of walking away (the action was unfinished) when I shouted. The shouting interrupted the walking away.
3 She walked away, then I shouted to her. The action of walking away was completed when the shout was made.
4 John got food poisoning, then he died (both finished actions).
5 He got food poisoning, and was in the process of dying from it (unfinished action).

6 The man was baking cakes (the action was unfinished), and his activity was interrupted when the children came home.
7 The children came home (completed action), and the man then made sandwiches for them. No action was interrupted.
8 He cooked dinner then the children came home. Both are finished actions.
9 The baby was crying, and I interrupted this by picking him up.
10 I picked up the baby (finished action) and then he started to cry.

B 1 drew, opened
2 dived, was drowning
3 climbed, shook
4 was writing, rang
5 was flying, caught
6 was burning, arrived

C The difference is that in sentence **a**, the money was already hidden when the police arrived; whereas in sentence **b**, the police arrived and then John hid the money. Sentence **b** shows John acted quickly when he realised the police were there. Sentence **a** means that the hiding of the money took place before the arrival of the police. John is in more danger of being arrested in sentence **b**. Sentences **c** and **d** mean the same.
If *before* is changed to *when* then the meaning of sentences may be different.

1 approached, realised, had not lowered
2 caught, bought
3 retired, had won
4 had shot, dragged
5 fell, broke

D

1	saw	11	knew
2	had had	12	took out
3	had obtained	13	unlocked
4	wanted	14	stepped
5	was looking	15	had been
6	walked/was walking	16	seemed
7	had	17	were
8	was watching	18	had not left
9	was imagining	19	was
10	told	20	had checked
21	began/was beginning	34	had stolen
22	had broken	35	was
23	had taken	36	was
24	was	37	had not checked
25	had left	38	opened
26	checked	39	realised
27	opened	40	had happened
28	had placed	41	had disappeared
29	was	42	was leaning
30	examined	43	heard
31	was	44	looked
32	had forced	45	were getting
33	had entered	46	had planned

Listening: Women to admire (page 138)

Notes on the text

Open University: an institution which allows people to study for a degree from home

on the dole: receiving unemployment benefit (colloq.)

take the bull by the horns: to tackle the subject (idiom)

Tapescript

INTERVIEWER: Is there anybody you particularly admire?

CLAIRE: Yes. I admire my mother an awful lot because she's brought my brother and I up on her own. Erm, we were about six I think when dad left. Oh I was six when dad left home, so she's been on her own now for twelve years. Within that twelve years she got an Open University degree. She was on the dole for eight years, no five years, and struggling to find employment for eight and … she's just gone through so much, but still kept me and my brother happy and comfortable and now she's come out of it and she's sort of getting her reward really because she's very happy in her work and she's earning a substantial amount of money and she's loving it.

MANDY: A friend of mine came round last night actually, so she's fresh in my mind but she would have been the first person I would have thought of if anybody asked me who do I admire a lot. And it's this friend: she … there's something about her, erm, I think what it is the word is bravery, courage and I don't necessarily mean physical courage, although I'm sure she is very brave in that way. It's, it's, it's more mental, erm, strength and where her real, her real bravery shows up among erm, of all her virtues erm, is that she … she will tell people what she thinks of them, in the nicest way if necessary or not if, if she feels she needs to say something … she cannot stand an un … erm … a dishonest situation between friends or, or even work colleagues, so if she feels that there's an atmosphere or that something needs sorting out she's the one who takes the bull by the horns and will actually broach the subject and go to somebody and say, 'Well, I'm sorry there's a problem here and I think we need to discuss it', and she will discuss it and she will sort it out. And the way she does it, it works, she doesn't do it in an aggressive way she just is able to put the cards on the table so to speak and be honest, and through her honesty other people feel they can be honest and say what they think, to the point where she doesn't like somebody she'll say, 'Well, I'm sorry but I really don't like you at all, but we either have a job to do and we have to do it or we are going to stop now.' And she has the bravery to say it. And I suppose I admire her particularly because I don't have that bravery and I think it's very admirable and she also is the soul of tact, at the same time as being able to, erm, cope with a difficult situation and actually speak out.

1 b
2 a, b
3 a
4 a
5 b
6 a
7 a
8 b
9 a

English in Use: (Grammar Notes **13.3**) (page 138)

1
1 memory
2 memorise
3 souvenirs
4 remind
5 reminder
6 memories
7 remembers/remembered
8 reminded
9 souvenir
10 remember

2
1 exhausting
2 tempting
3 surprising
4 frustrated
5 terrifying
6 fascinated
7 boring
8 interested
9 tiring
10 scared

Reading: *Custer's Last Stand* (page 139)

Notes on the text

George Armstrong Custer (1830–1876) was a US soldier. After a brilliant career as a cavalry commander in the American Civil War he served in campaigns against the Indian tribes of the Great Plains. He was defeated by a combined force of Cheyenne and Sioux at Little Big Horn on 25 June 1876. His defeat came as a great shock to the American establishment. There are many books and films about Custer and many people regard him as a hero. Others, however, criticise his attacks on defenceless Indian villages and his incompetence at Little Big Horn.

treaty: law

prospector: person who explores a region looking for gold

Sample answer

Since the beginning of settlement in North America, the Indian tribes had been forced to move away from their lands. The pressure mounted on them in the 1840s and 1850s, and there was an awareness that the Indians were losing their hunting grounds. One of their leaders, Chief Sitting Bull, was angry at the treatment they were receiving from the government, which was now supporting the rights of gold-prospectors in the sacred lands in Dakota. General Custer was sent to deal with the resistance. He was confident he would succeed, but the major part of his troops were driven off by the Indians, and he and the remaining troops were killed in the Battle of Little Big Horn. Although the Indians won the battle, the defeat led the government to use stronger measures against the Indians, who lost their independence.

Reading: *Living with my own legend* (page 140)

A *Notes on the text*

Boris Becker: German tennis player born in 1967, the youngest winner of the men's singles at Wimbledon at the age of 17 in 1985 and winner of the title again in the following year. World Championship Tennis champion and the Masters Champion in 1988.

B 1 H 2 B 3 F 4 G 5 A 6 D 7 E

Talking Points (page 141)

Section 1

The photograph on the left shows an athlete being mobbed by fans who are taking his photograph and asking for his autograph. The photograph on the right is Queen Beatrix of the Netherlands greeting the public and touching someone's hand.

Section 2

This section provides students with the opportunity to discuss the figures they admire, how they express that admiration, and what makes these people popular.

Listening: *Oliver Cromwell* (page 142)

Tapescript

PRESENTER: Today, in our series about important historical figures, we look at Oliver Cromwell, born 1599, died 1658, country gentleman, army commander, Member of Parliament, Lord Protector of the Commonwealth of England, Scotland and Ireland, and finally military dictator. To some people he is a villain; to others a hero. What was he in reality? I shall be asking three writers to give their opinion of Oliver Cromwell.

FIRST WRITER: Oliver Cromwell was against the King, whom he sentenced to death; he was against the Monarchy; he was against the Church of England. He said he was for the rights of the people, for democracy: but he became a dictator. He was responsible for the Civil War which divided the country; members of the same family fought against each other, son against father, brother against brother. In the end he achieved nothing. I think the Civil War could have been avoided. The Monarchy returned in 1660, anyway, two years after Cromwell's death.

SECOND WRITER: I disagree. Cromwell did not want a civil war. He did not wish to destroy the Monarchy. It was the King, Charles I, who wanted to rule without Parliament and who tried to take away the rights of the people. Cromwell was a religious man and a democrat, who tried to defend the rights of the elected Parliament. He kept England, Scotland and Ireland united and made them strong. He fought against religious fanatics and prevented the return of absolute monarchy, of the absolute power of the King. His dream did not come true in his lifetime. But the Glorious Revolution of 1688, which put William of Orange on the throne of England, was only possible because of the English Revolution led by Cromwell.

THIRD WRITER: I think that Cromwell was an ambitious man, after all he thought of himself as God's Englishman. He was a fanatic who took power in the name of God and the people. He prevented the King from becoming an absolute monarch, but he nearly became King himself. And he turned against the common people who had supported him. He defended only the rights of men of property. He killed soldiers, priests and innocent people in Ireland. So, in my opinion, Cromwell can't be called either a hero or a villain: like most great military and political leaders, he is both.

1 The seventeenth century.
2 Charles I.
3 No.
4 1660.
5 The rights of the people.
6 England, Scotland and Ireland.
7 William of Orange.
8 He killed soldiers, priests and innocent people.
9 First writer – against; second writer – for; third writer – neutral.

Writing: *Biography* (page 142)

C Students should include as much information as possible in their biographies and maintain a clear narrative line. Ask students to use the biography of Marilyn Monroe and also the tapescript of the listening passage on Oliver Cromwell (page 75 Teacher's Book) as models for their chosen biographies.

English in Use (page 143)

1

1	hold	9	number
2	biased	10	circulation
3	lack	11	mass
4	news	12	quality
5	articles	13	keep
6	editorial	14	reviews
7	earn/make	15	which
8	different/various		

2 Phrasal verbs

1	called in	6	call for
2	call on	7	called out
3	called away	8	called for
4	called off	9	call back
5	call round	10	called up

3 Word-formation

1	boyish	6	successful
2	harmful	7	girlish
3	handful	8	thoughtful
4	childish	9	mouthful
5	careful	10	teaspoonful

unit 14 VICTIMS AND VILLAINS

Lead-in (page 144)

1 The top photograph shows a man wearing a balaclava looking aggressive. Elicit from students nouns such as *yobbo (colloq.), thug, petty-criminal.*

The bottom photograph shows a bedroom which has been burgled and ransacked. Clothes and papers are strewn all over the floor and the chair is overturned. The burglars have obviously gone through the wardrobe and chest of drawers looking for valuables. Elicit from students vocabulary such as *to be burgled, to leave the house in complete chaos, to hide the valuables, papers strewn over the floor, to have a burglar alarm fitted.*

In everyday life, probably petty theft, mugging, car theft and burglary are the most troublesome crimes.

2

1	e	6	f
2	a	7	h
3	i	8	b
4	c	9	j
5	d	10	g

3

1	committed	11	evidence
2	arrested	12	verdict
3	charged	13	acquit
4	bail	14	convict
5	accused	15	found
6	custody	16	sentence
7	court	17	fine
8	defence	18	prison
9	plead	19	crime
10	witnesses		

Reading: *Dressing to kill leads to murder in Chicago* (page 146)

A Certain items, for example a particular brand of trainers or designer labels, can become extremely fashionable for young people to wear. Sometimes clothes become associated with a particular group of people who have a certain lifestyle. Invite students to think of topical examples.

Elicit vocabulary such as *to be hip/trendy* (colloq.), *to be 'in'* (colloq.), *to wear a (designer) label.*

B
1 a macabre connotation
2 fatal
3 catching on
4 logos
5 all the rage
6 accosted him
7 spotted
8 put it another way
9 hang on to
10 blow him away
11 related to
12 implemented

C
1 In this context it means that people are wearing clothes that other people are prepared to kill them for. It normally refers to a glamorous way of dressing by women which is intended to make a big impact on men.
2 Young people who do not want to pay high prices for fashionable clothes, kill people who have bought them. The desire to be fashionable themselves makes them kill.
3 He was shot in the back while trying to run away from his attacker.
4 They began last autumn.
5 The 'wrong' colour shoes would be shoes that, perhaps accidentally, indicated allegiance to a rival gang (in Los Angeles the two largest gangs are the 'Bloods' who wear red and the 'Crips' who wear blue).
6 The reasons are the desire to have fashionable clothes and, in some cases, gang or team loyalties.
7 The Detroit Board of Education is going to implement a schools' dress code.

Grammar: *revision of conditionals* (Grammar Notes **5.1**, **12.2**, **14.1**) (page 147)

A
1 f
2 g
3 e
4 a
5 h
6 c
7 i
8 b
9 d

(Grammar Notes **14.2**)

B
1 Unless you are a member, …
2 … unless you produce a medical certificate.
3 … unless traffic lights are installed.
4 Unless we replace these old windows, …
5 Unless he is caught quickly, …

Many answers are possible. These are examples.

6 Unless you have passed the appropriate exams, …
7 Unless you have a visa, …
8 Unless you have a cheque card, …
9 Unless the government does something soon, …
10 Unless it is reinforced, …

C 8, 11, 15 are incorrect. Correct versions would be:
8 If I helped you now, I know you wouldn't help me later.
11 If I dug in that spot, would I find the treasure?
15 If the sun shone, we would go for a picnic.

Listening: *Being arrested* (page 148)

Tapescript

INTERVIEWER: Have you ever been arrested?

REBECCA: Oh dear, yes I'm afraid I have, and it wasn't a very nice experience! Erm it was my birthday and I went out with a friend and we had a meal and half a bottle of wine each with the meal and then we went onto a jazz club and I had one more drink there and er … came out at about half past one in the morning. And I was driving home and I was chatting to my friend and not paying sufficient attention to the road and at a certain point er, in the middle of Soho where there are a lot of little streets that I'm not very familiar with, I was about to turn right. And at the very last minute I realised that it was a one-way street and in fact it was a no right turn so I was preparing to turn the wheel right round so that I could turn left which was the correct way to go, and then I noticed there were two policemen standing on the corner just a few feet away and they were witnessing me doing this … what looked like a, a strange manoeuvre and they signalled for me to stop and of course they said, 'Have you been drinking?' and I had to admit, yes I … I, I had been drinking, so they said, 'Well if you don't mind, we'd like to … er … like you to take a breathalyser test,' and they produced this er, small contraption it looks rather like a … a Walkman and you have to blow into it. I think it's … erm … well, there's, there's a light that comes on when you've blown sufficient air into it and then you have to wait for, I believe it's 30 seconds, to see whether a green light comes on in which case they arrest you, and in fact that's … that's what happened. Just before the, the 30 seconds was up the green light came on, so the policewoman reached out and touched my shoulder and said all these special words that they have to say, er, which is the formal way of arresting people, and they also have to touch you while they're doing this, and er I, I was really quite shocked and er … then because these two policemen had been on foot I had to go with them to the police station, so they er contacted the nearest er police station and they sent a van to collect me … er … because I had to go then and have another test at the police station – the breathalyser on the pavement was sufficient for them to arrest me but it wasn't sufficient for them to, to charge me with a drink-driving offence. So, erm I got into this van and erm … then I suddenly heard a crackling over their radio and I couldn't hear what they were … they heard but the reply was, 'No, I'm sorry we can't come at the moment we've got a prisoner on board,' and I suddenly realised, well, that was me! I was the prisoner! And I thought this was really rather amusing and I wanted to laugh but I thought it wouldn't look good if I laughed so I, I, I tried not to but er … yes, this, that … that struck me as being rather funny. So we got to the police station and er they had to fill in all these forms er, all kind of details about me and where I lived, and I, I can't remember exactly but I mean they were very polite and very nice about it and they explained then that I had to blow into another machine that they had there, an enormous machine and er, this gave a very er accurate reading apparently and if I was er, above 35 they would then charge me with a drink-driving offence. Well I can't remember what the 35 exactly erm, related to but that was some kind of limit. Anyway, er, they said I could have two goes just in case er one of them wasn't quite accurate, erm, and so I, I blew into this … I believe they called it an intoxometer, and I was quite nervous because I really couldn't decide whether you know, I had had too much to drink or not and er … so the first reading was eight and the second reading was seven, in other words it was nowhere near the limit. … so obviously I was very, very relieved but then I thought, and I said to them, but what about that breathalyser I took on the pavement, er obviously, that machine was really, really inaccurate because erm, according to that, I, I was very close to the limit and er … which is obviously why you arrested me and now, erm, OK it was maybe three quarters of an hour later, but the reading was very, very low and in fact they didn't really have an explanation for that and all they could say was 'Well, most of the people we arrest really are drunk.' Er but of course in my case it wasn't true, er but I've er always been very, very careful about drinking and driving after that and I never have more than two or at very most, three units so that I'm absolutely clear how much er how much alcohol I've drunk because … I don't want to get arrested again!

1	birthday	9	van
2	half a bottle	10	bigger
3	jazz club	11	more accurate
4	1.30	12	thirty-five
5	right	13	eight
6	two	14	seven
7	thirty	15	forty-five
8	green	16	three

English in Use (page 148)

1 Rob, steal (Grammar Notes **14.3**)

1	robbed	6	robbers
2	robbery	7	stealing
3	stolen	8	stolen
4	stole	9	robbed
5	robbed	10	stealing

2 Fault, blame (Grammar Notes **14.4**)

A 1 The accident was Richard's fault.
2 The crash was the pilot's fault.
3 This crime was partly the victim's fault.
4 It's not my fault!
5 It's not my fault at all./I will not accept that I am at fault in any way.

B 1 The other driver was to blame for the accident.
2 People blamed the manager for the heavy losses./People said the manager was to blame.
3 The cyclist agreed that he was partly to blame.
4 Peter is not to blame!
5 You are not to blame in any way.

Reading: *Lessons on a life of crime* (page 149)

A You can consider such things as punishment as a deterrent, punishment for punishment's sake, rehabilitation, skills training. As for the causes of crime, encourage students to consider greed, poverty, malice, moral depravity, etc. In the United Kingdom, young people under the age of ten cannot be charged with a criminal offence. Between the ages of fourteen and twenty, offenders may be sent to a youth custody centre. Offenders under the age of twenty-one cannot be sent to an ordinary prison. Young people under the age of fourteen who have committed an offence can also be taken into care by the local authority.

Elicit from students vocabulary such as *to serve a prison sentence*, *to be taken into custody*, *to go to gaol*, *punishment as deterrent*, *to get a criminal record*.

Notes on the text

borstal: the old term for a youth custody centre, named after the village of Borstal in Kent, where the first such centre was established in 1908

parole licence: to be 'on parole', enables you to live outside of prison even though you have not finished your sentence

B 1	sentence	6	traces
2	parole	7	conscience
3	criminal record	8	embark on
4	redeem himself	9	shuffling
5	thick		

C 1	False	5	True
2	False	6	True
3	True	7	True
4	True		

Reading: *Two armed raiders killed in shoot-out with police* (page 146)

A Draw students' attention to the map which clarifies what happens in the story. Note that British policemen are not normally armed but have guns available for special duties. Rayners Lane is in the north-west of London.

Notes on the text

balaclava: a close fitting woollen hat that covers the head, neck and part of the face

sawn-off shotgun: a shotgun (normally used for hunting birds and rabbits) which has had the barrel cut short to make it easy to hide under a jacket

B

1	marksmen	8	alley
2	courageously	9	opened fire
3	inevitable response	10	staking out
4	ramming	11	oblivious
5	girder	12	regretted
6	reversing	13	extended
7	abandoned		

C In order to answer these questions students must interpret the text in such a way that they understand what is not explicitly stated. The following answers are suggestions only.

1 They probably stole the van, the two getaway cars and the girder, and purchased the guns illegally. They may have had inside information about the post office. It is possible that they were misled by false information coming from the police.
2 Probably very angry because there was no money there.
3 What they really said is probably unrepeatable in the classroom but they must have decided to abandon their plan and make for the getaway car.
4 They drove away and then abandoned the car and ran down an alley. When they saw the second group of policemen, they opened fire.
5 It is possible that they knew everything. Obviously they knew the time and place of the raid. They knew the robbers would be armed and therefore were armed themselves. They must have known where the second getaway car was.
6 They were the other side of the bridge, where the second getaway car was.
7 He thought he was watching a film being made. He didn't realise he was in danger.

D These writing tasks should be written in the first person, using past tenses. Students can use their imaginations and add details to the facts in the reading text.

Talking Points (page 151)

Section 1

Contrasts or ironies in the poem are the fact that it is a fine *day* but the middle of the *night*, the men who were fighting were *already dead*, they were *back to back* yet *were looking at each other*, they fought with *swords* yet killed each other with *guns*.

Section 2

In considering these moral issues, students should bear in mind such factors as accidents, carelessness, deliberate intention to harm, age, deliberate planning and premeditation, spontaneous behaviour, sudden loss of temper, damage to property, injury to people, ignorance of the law.

Elicit from students various forms of punishment such as *the death penalty*, *life imprisonment*, *some years or months in prison*, *a fine*, *paying compensation to the victim*, *losing one's job*, *being told off*.

Section 3

The photograph shows a released prisoner standing outside gaol about to start a new life. Discussions could focus on hope, a new future, returning home, seeing your family and old friends *or* the fact that prospects for reintegration into society after serving a long prison sentence are not good, that society often rejects these with a prison record and many companies will be unwilling to employ him.

Listening: *Witnessing a crime* (page 152)

Notes on the text

Sainsbury's: a well known, large supermarket company

Tapescript

SPEAKER 1: Well erm … I … it was erm, it was about seven o'clock at night and er, it was getting quite dark and er, I got off the bus which is just round the corner from my house and as I turned the corner a group of about five, five or six, erm I don't know, like teenagers rushed past me, absolutely sort of like stormed past me almost knocked me over erm and I thought you know, teenagers you know having a good time running about. Well, of course I went, erm, went into my flat, well down, down the stairs to the door, and it was open and I thought my flatmate had er, arrived back early, left the door open. Well of course he hadn't, and there was nobody in there, erm … the door was open. Of course as I moved in, the place was in a complete state of chaos. Everything was on the floor, drawers had been just opened, stuff thrown around all over the place, the whole place was in a complete state of erm well, chaos really. Erm and of course I realised the moment that I saw this situation, I thought, 'It was them!' And I thought I thought, right I mean, I didn't think of anything else but running after them, but then I thought, 'No it's too late, they'll have got away anyway.' I mean I … I didn't know any of their faces … I couldn't recognise any of them or anything, erm, but the ridiculous thing was that nothing was stolen, that was the extraordinary thing, there was absolutely nothing missing. And er, I just thought, 'Well what a waste.' You know, at least they could've stolen something, made it worthwhile.

SPEAKER 2: I was in erm, a block of flats waiting for a friend. I was actually in the corridor and I was on the second floor, and I knew he was due to come back. So I just waited in the corridor and I looked out of the window and there was er the street below and parked cars and so on, and there were these er, two teenagers. I suppose they must've been sixteen, one was black and one was white and they were walking up and down past these cars, having a look in. And it was sort of dusk time and er I was fascinated by this and then … they worked as a team, one had a very large hammer, a lump hammer I mean, one of those for knocking down walls. Erm, they'd selected the cars they wanted to … there were about three they selected, one went along with the lump hammer bashing in the sidelight window of these three cars and the other put the hand in, took out the bag, three bags, off down the street, I should think it was all over in about a minute. And I … I rang the police but erm, and I had to give a statement later. But I mean, it was far too late and I couldn't recognise them from that distance. Nobody ever got their property back, I imagine. It all happened so quickly.

SPEAKER 3: I remember one particular day I was shopping in Sainsbury's and erm I saw this man, he had a Sainsbury's basket in one hand and his shopping bag on his arm, and he put a tin of sardines in his basket and he put a tin of pilchards in his bag, and I saw him do that. I looked at him fascinated, and then he walked on a bit further and he put a tin of ham in his bag, and I felt so hot and embarrassed. I hadn't done anything, but I was I, I was following him round Sainsbury's just watching what he was doing. And there was a small item going in his basket and a bigger item going in his bag and I must've walked, well practically all round the counters, watching this man and then all of a sudden I stopped and realised that people would think I was with him, because I was just watching and I wasn't shopping, I was just following him around and seeing what he was doing, and you have to think, are you going to report him, or what are you going to do, you know? It's ever such a difficult situation to be in and an embarrassing one. So in the end I walked to the checkout, put my basket down and walked out of the shop. I never did any shopping, and I stood outside and I waited for this man to come out and he came through the checkout, paid for his few items in the basket and he walked out and Sainsbury's never caught him, then I went in and did my shopping. I mean that man had that effect on me, and I hadn't done anything! But seeing someone else do it, is, is you know, you don't know whether to report them or what to do, it's very difficult.

1	Speakers 1, 2	8	Speaker 1
2	Speakers 1, 2	9	Speakers 1, 2
3	Speaker 2	10	Speakers 1, 3
4	Speaker 3	11	Speakers 1, 3
5	Speakers 1, 2	12	Speaker 2
6	Speaker 1, 2	13	Speaker 3
7	Speakers 1, 2, 3		

Writing: *Story writing* (page 152)

In Paper 2 of the FCE examination there is a question in which the first or last sentence of a story is given for students to continue.

A The first sentences are taken from:

1 *1984* (George Orwell)
2 *One Hundred Years of Solitude* (Gabriel Garcia Marquez)
3 *Anna Karenina* (Leo Tolstoy)
4 *Kidnapped* (Robert Louis Stevenson)
5 *The Good Soldier* (Ford Madox Ford)
6 *Pride and Prejudice* (Jane Austen)
7 *Darkness at Noon* (Arthur Koestler)
8 *The Trial* (Franz Kafka)

1	f, b	5	f
2	a, e	6	g
3	g	7	a, c
4	d, a	8	a, c, f

English in Use (page 153)

1 Phrasal verbs

1	make up for	6	keep up with
2	face up to	7	got rid of
3	get away with	8	come up with
4	come forward with	9	made off with
5	caught up with	10	broke out of

2 In prison, in the prison (Grammar Notes **14.5**)

1	from hospital	6	in court
2	to the hospital	7	in the court
3	from prison	8	in a prison
4	to hospital	9	in prison
5	in hospital	10	to prison

3 Word-formation

1	punctuality	5	kindness
2	deafness	6	illness
3	seriousness	7	formality
4	stupidity	8	popularity

unit 15 LIES, TRICKS AND DECEIT

Lead-in (page 154)

1 The photographs show two cases where deception is employed in common situations.

The photograph below shows a magician sawing a man in half, and like most shows of magic is a way of deceiving the audience. The photograph above shows an attempt at smuggling by lining a suitcase with a false bottom.

Students should discuss other aspects of deception they encounter in everyday life such as *cheating in exams, altering the mileage on a car, lying about your age to obtain something you want, misleading people about your background, telling a lie/fib, misleading someone, playing a trick on someone, conning someone into doing something, two-timing someone.*

2

1	posed	6	betraying
2	disguised	7	cheats
3	forged	8	tricked
4	deceive	9	impersonating
5	suspected	10	misled

3

1	counterfeit	6	swindler
2	fake	7	fraud
3	false	8	espionage
4	artificial	9	deception
5	hoax	10	lie

Reading: *Moment of truth* (page 156)

A Students should be encouraged to recount their own experiences of theft, whether at school, at home or on the street. They should consider fully how they felt as a result of the theft, and whether they thought the thief had come to justice. They could also consider how the thief felt.

B
1 the thing I own that I like the most
2 lost
3 thought to have taken the objects
4 expensive items
5 valuable objects dating from the past
6 I used to read aloud to her
7 not to be found
8 a student who starts studying in higher education when older than 26

C
1 A tortoiseshell hairslide, pens, purses, a silver box, a ring, a framed mirror.
2 They liked each other and had a good relationship.
3 The old lady was blind, and Jennifer thought because of this that she would not realise what was going on.
4 She left Jennifer three objects in her will.
5 Yes, she clearly did, as she gave to Jennifer the objects she knew she had stolen.
6 She was shocked.
7 She didn't steal again, improved her educational level by going to college and now works with the elderly.

Grammar: *indirect speech* (1) (Grammar Notes **15.1**) (page 157)

A The six changes that have been made are:

word order: 'what time will you get here' becomes 'what time he would get there' i.e. verb + subject becomes subject + verb.

verb form: 'will you get here' becomes 'would get'.

pronouns: 'you' becomes 'he'.

time words: 'tomorrow' becomes 'the following day'

place words: 'here' becomes 'there'.

punctuation: speech marks and question mark are dropped.

B
1 Sarah asked Sally when she would give her the tickets.
2 Michael asked me what I would say at the meeting the next day.
3 Victoria asked David where he would put his new bookcase.
4 William asked Jane if she would be staying in that village until the following day.
5 Robert asked John if he would come by himself or whether he would bring his family.
6 Lucy asked Arnold if he would help her move the filing cabinets.

C
1 Change in word order, change in verb form, dropping of speech marks and question mark.
2 Change in word order, change in verb form – 'do you know' becomes 'if he knew', insertion of 'if' instead of 'do', change of pronouns, dropping of speech marks and question mark.
3 Change of verb form, change of word order, insertion of 'if', change of pronouns, dropping of speech marks and question mark.
4 Change of verb form, change of word order, change of pronouns, dropping of speech marks and question mark.

D
1 Maria asked me what she could do to improve things.
2 I asked the stewardess where the emergency exit was.
3 I asked Mary why she saw (had seen) a lawyer.
4 Tony asked me where I had put the passports.
5 John asked Lisa what she wanted to do the next day.
6 Julia asked Bernard if he liked spicy food.
7 Mrs Osborne asked me if I (had) enjoyed the performance.
8 Louise asked Charles if he was going to her party the following week.
9 The shop assistant asked me if I could wait two more days.
10 Jenny asked Lucy if her brother always visited her on Saturdays.

Listening: *The great tortoise mystery* (page 158)

Tapescript

SPEAKER: Well, I remember a story about a practical joke which was told to me by a friend of mine. It is about someone who he was at university with and this person, I think his name was Peter, rented a room in a large house, as did a few other students … and the landlady lived on the premises. And apparently the landlady was a very kind-hearted lady and she was very fond of animals. She had a couple of cats, and a dog and er, she kept rabbits as well and she read a lot of books about animals, always watched the nature programmes on television. Well, anyway, Peter decided to give his landlady a present and he went to a pet shop and bought a small tortoise and gave it to her. She was very pleased with it and put it in her garden. A tortoise was a good choice, of course, because its hard shell would protect it from the cats and the dog. Well, erm, the landlady started to feed the tortoise on a special mix of vegetables which she prepared and within a few days, to everyone's astonishment, the tortoise had doubled in size – it really was twice as big. And then after a few more days the tortoise had doubled in size yet again. By this time, the newspapers and local radio had got to hear about it and the landlady was interviewed by journalists and everyone wanted to know about this special mix of vegetables that she fed to the tortoise, that had made it grow so fast and people were talking about scientifically analysing the tortoise's food to find out what the magic ingredient was.

What had happened, of course, was that Peter had secretly removed the small tortoise and replaced it with a medium-sized one and then removed that and replaced it with a large one. Since tortoises look much the same, people thought the same one was growing fast. Anyway, Peter couldn't find a really big tortoise with which to continue, so he removed the large tortoise and replaced it with the medium tortoise and then, a few days later, he took the medium tortoise away and put back the small tortoise. So it seemed to the landlady that her tortoise was now shrinking, so she started to feed it much more food in the hope that it would start growing again. At this point, Peter realised that the tortoise was being given so much food that it might die of overeating so he had to confess what he had done and er, he told the landlady the truth. Surprisingly, perhaps, she forgave him and let him stay in the house. Peter gave her the other two tortoises, so, since she loved animals, perhaps she was pleased to have three of them in her garden. I suppose Peter was lucky in a way, that his landlady was so good-natured, because sometimes people get very angry if you play tricks on them.

A

1	False	4	False
2	False	5	False
3	True	6	True

English in Use (page 158)

1 Prepositions

1	from	6	for, to
2	about	7	into
3	in	8	from
4	about	9	to
5	to	10	out

2

1	were	9	✓
2	✓	10	she
3	deep	11	by
4	it	12	for
5	being	13	than
6	✓	14	been
7	did	15	the
8	into		

Reading: *Four years' jail and a ruined life for conman, 18* (page 159)

Confidence tricksters trick people into doing something they want, such as giving them money or favours. They work by using basic elements of human behaviour.

	Answers – text a	**Answers – text b**
1	18	18
2	16	16
3	an international investments advisor	a City stockbroker
4	£200,000	£214,000
5	mortgage: £466,000 house: price not given	mortgage: £466,000 house: £516,000
6	he used his father's credit card; he swindled a former teacher and the teacher's girlfriend out of £13,000	he used his father's credit card; he swindled a former teacher out of £13,000
7	hired private jets; drove Ferraris and Porsches; went to nightclubs; went shopping in Harrods and spent £1,700; spent £11,000 in other shops, restaurants and garages	hired private jets; wined and dined girlfriends; rented a suite at a Brighton hotel
8	no information	his father wrote to solicitors and accountants telling them how old his son was
9	no information	that he was out of touch with reality; he was in need of psychiatric treatment; he was an inadequate boy without any sense of reality and he could not have hoped to get away with it
10	he was utterly selfish and completely ruthless; he showed all the typical symptoms of a conman, telling sophisticated lies to victims, cleverly adapted to suit circumstances; he told lie after lie in order to get people's money so that he could squander it on self-indulgent pleasure to gratify his gambler's desire to speculate	he was utterly selfish and completely ruthless; he did not accept that he was a character believing in a fantasy world; the sentence reflected the overall wickedness of his crimes; he showed all the typical symptoms of a conman, telling sophisticated lies to victims
11	a four-year jail sentence	four years in a young offenders' institution

Reading: *The Tichborne case* (page 160)

A Students should discuss cases of imposters and people impersonating others. They should discuss the pressures that make someone do this such as *the need to escape*, *the desire for personal gain*, *the wish for revenge*, *to pose as someone*.

B 1 D 2 C 3 C 4 C 5 C

Talking Points (page 161)

Section 1

The advertisements show a light which uses solar energy to work, a travelling-set of encyclopaedias and a lamp which changes to the colour of the room in which it is placed. The advertisements come from a Barclays Bank publicity campaign to promote their business advice and loans department. They are intended to amuse and are a 'play' on misleading advertisements. Beyond discussing the advertisements provided, students could consider other advertisements that aim to mislead.

Listening: *Deceiving people* (page 162)

Notes on the text

This is Your Life!: this is a reference to a well-known British TV programme of the same name which invites showbiz personalities and other people to appear on the programme to meet people who have been important in their lives

Tapescript

MANDY: I have to confess that I did tell a big lie, a whopper, and of course crime doesn't pay, and I got into trouble. And erm, I was a student and erm, you know, I didn't have very much money and I wanted to go out one night and I didn't have enough money to get to wherever I was going, so …

JAMES: Sounds like an excuse already!

MANDY: Hmmm … that's right, (your honour your honour), so I decided well I'll just … you know, I won't pay my tube fare, and actually I have to admit that I had been doing this for about two weeks, because my grant had run out, that's the excuse, and erm, er I arrived at Leicester Square tube station and this gentleman stopped me and said, 'Madam can I see your ticket?' and I did have a ticket but erm, it was out of date and you know, I started to bluff and I thought 'I must say something sensible' and very stupidly I said, 'I've come from Charing Cross,' which is one tube station before Leicester Square, which, you know, basically if you're going to deceive somebody you should do it properly and I did it very badly. And had I said I'd come from a longer journey he might have perhaps believed me, but …

JAMES: Hmmm … the station could have been closed …

MANDY: Well yes, but I mean it wasn't closed it was absolutely and definitely open. There were lots of people on duty and I … I'm afraid I didn't lie very well, and I ended up erm, confessing to my lie which again you must never do, you know, always stick to your lie, and erm, I didn't even give a false name and address. I gave my own name and address. And of course I got a letter and I ended up going to Bow Street Court.

JAMES: Oh!

MANDY: I mean I could have chosen not to but I decided I quite wanted to go and I had to pay £50 which was a lot of money then.

ALL: Yes, hmm.

JAMES: Well, I mean I, I, I … I did, I must admit I also must confess to deceiving somebody pretty, pretty completely actually, and I did it very successfully, erm but it was really all nice in the end because it was erm … I arranged a big kind of reunion, we had a favourite teacher at school, really nice guy. Erm and erm, we were just about to leave, this was the … he was about to leave in fact, leave the school and we were about to leave as the last year in the school, and erm we decided to do a big kind of reunion thing for him, erm, but it was a … to be a complete surprise and it was to be on his last day as a teacher and he was going to do the normal school assembly in the morning, and me and a friend spent weeks and weeks gathering people together from his past like … from like you know twelve years away. And my friend was going to present the whole thing as a big show, erm with a … and she erm had a big red book er and er to do it in the proper manner, you know, and erm … and just as he was about to finish the assembly the curtains on stage went back and she stepped forward and she said to him, his name was Mr Gateshill, she said, 'Mr Gateshill, you thought this was going to be an easy final assembly for you but in fact, Paul Gateshill, This is Your Life!' And she did … the whole music went up, we had music, we had star guests, we had all these old er friends from school, we had the lot, people who he hadn't seen for fifteen years, and he was completely, completely fooled …

MANDY: What was his reaction?

JAMES: I mean he was completely flabbergasted, and at the end, at the end he loved it, he absolutely loved it but he was … but he sort of hated it at the end, at the same time.

MANDY: Yes, yes.

1 True
2 False
3 False
4 True
5 False
6 False
7 True
8 True
9 True
10 False
11 False
12 True
13 True
14 False
15 False

Writing: *A letter giving advice to a friend* (page 162)

Students should pay great attention to the tone of this letter, which is a difficult one to write.

English in Use (page 163)

1

1	to	11	convince
2	an	12	been
3	round/around	13	at
4	How	14	dealing
5	before	15	what
6	trained	16	looked
7	not	17	one
8	put	18	admit
9	later	19	instead
10	past	20	faces

2 Phrasal verbs

1	cut up	5	cut off
2	cut out	6	cut out
3	cut down	7	cut down on
4	cut off	8	cuts in

3 Word-formation

1	privacy	6	necessity
2	certainty	7	fluency
3	anxiety	8	variety
4	efficiency	9	Curiosity
5	accuracy	10	tragedy

Exam Practice 3 (page 164)

1 1 G 2 D 3 A 4 F 5 I 6 B 7 H

2

1 Mary had no money left at the end of term.
2 The carpenter says it's the best he can do.
3 Jenny was robbed of her handbag in the street.
4 What is your explanation for/of the damage to this car?
5 John said that her performance had made a big impression on him.
6 The sailors are in danger of being swept away by the huge waves.
7 Nobody spoke/said/uttered a word until the music stopped.
8 Jack's knee was injured as a result of playing too much football.
9 A sea wall provides the town with protection/protection for the town against high seas.
10 We made many complaints but nothing was done.

3

1 The weatherman's advice to drivers was not to travel.
2 There was great loss of life in the storm.
3 You cannot survive (for) more than four days without water.
4 Sally had difficulty (in) completing her test on time.
5 'Checking these documents is not my responsibility,' said Martin.
6 Although he was injured he managed to climb the mountain.
7 Tom said that he had stolen the money.
8 The time machine appeared/seemed to be an ordinary car.
9 It's not worth repairing this old bicycle.
10 Give John your mobile phone number in case he needs to contact you.

4

1	B	9	D
2	B	10	B
3	D	11	A
4	D	12	B
5	C	13	D
6	C	14	A
7	A	15	C
8	A		

5 **Listening** (page 167)

Tapescript

1 …so he told me he had built one himself at home in his garage but I didn't believe him because I thought it was impossible to build one of those by yourself, but he insisted that I come and see it. So I went and it was quite small, about three metres long, and there was only room for one person inside. He said it could go down to 60 metres and travel at about 15 kilometres per hour and it was easy to steer. It was perfectly safe, he said, but I didn't think so. I'd be worried about being able to breathe.

2 SPEAKER 1: Can I have your card, please?

SPEAKER 2: My card? I'm going to pay cash.

SPEAKER 1: No, I mean your membership card. We only sell to members.

SPEAKER 2: Oh, I am a member. Been a member for years.

SPEAKER 1: Yes, but we have to see everyone's card. We have to run them through the machine, which checks them against an up-to-date list of members.

3 My grandmother bought it years ago. It used to hang in her kitchen. It was very dirty but you could just make out some tables and chairs in a room. Anyway, we decided to have it cleaned, which cost a fortune, and afterwards it looked completely different. You could even tell the time on the clock on the wall, and before you couldn't even see the clock. The man who cleaned it pointed out the signature to us. Well, as soon as I saw it I knew I had to sell.

4 I've been entering the competition for about six years now. Last year I came second and the year before second and once I came third, so this year, naturally I was hoping ... Well, the judges made their decision and it wasn't to be, not even a place this time. I thought it was my best entry ever ... I'm glad it's all over, anyway.

5 I really don't think it's suitable for you. It's extremely violent and you wouldn't be able to see it at the cinema. They won't serve you in the shop either – you're too young. You have to be over eighteen to rent videos from that shop. Maybe your friends at school have seen it but that doesn't mean you have to. I'm not getting it for you to watch.

6 We were supposed to play them on Saturday afternoon. We weren't looking forward to it because every time we played them before, we lost, usually quite badly. But we had been training hard, hoping to achieve a victory at last, or at least do better than in previous games. We needn't have bothered. The match was postponed at the last minute.

7 I'm sorry to interrupt you when you are all working so hard but there is an important change to number 37. You can add the letter D after the letter B and then go back and check the ones you have already done and include this change where necessary. Yes, I know it's a bit of extra work and I'm sorry about that, but you've worked so fast we are well ahead of schedule so you won't lose any time.

8 WOMAN: ... so we would really like you to come to the meeting on Tuesday.

MAN: It's very difficult, in fact it's simply impossible. I can't make Tuesday at all.

WOMAN: Well, we could change it to Wednesday, if you can come then.

MAN: Well, Wednesday would be better but ... yes, I could come on Wednesday but to be perfectly honest I would prefer not to. I really don't think it is necessary for me to attend. There is no reason why you shouldn't hold the meeting without me.

1 C 2 B 3 A 4 C 5 A 6 C 7 B 8 A

6 Listening (page 167)

Tapescript

Katherine: When I was a child my parents used to take me to Devon a lot, and there was this lovely little village in Devon called Clovelly, which is sort of situated on a very steep hill, and all clusters of little cottages and very beautiful and at the bottom of the hill there's the sea and the harbour and it was lovely, and it was totally unspoilt and it was just great, and I used to love it. Anyway, many years later, about twenty years later, I was telling a friend of mine about this and I went on and on and on about how nice this village was in the middle of Devon, and how we should go and look at it and so we did, we made this special expedition and we went off to it and we got there and I was horrified – there was just a big concrete car park with an enormous building, with like a little tollgate and you had to pay to go in and there were all little shops inside it. When you went through the complex and paid then you were allowed to enter the village and they were shipping people in, sort of ten or twenty at a time because then it wouldn't get too full. And I understand why they did it, they did it to protect the village and to preserve it and to stop too many tourists visiting it, but it was just completely ruined in my idea, with this big set of shops in front of it and this place you have to pass through to go in and when you got inside it was just full of tourists, there were no real people left there. It was really depressing, and I was very disappointed and so was my friend.

1 parents
2 on a hill
3 boats
4 friend
5 car park/building
6 pay
7 10 or 20
8 tourists
9 real people
10 disappointed/depressed

unit 16 A THING OF BEAUTY IS A JOY FOREVER

Lead-in (page 168)

1 The photographs show a Gaudí building, a Rodin sculpture entitled 'Hands' and Léger's 'Les Constructeurs'.

Gaudí: (1852–1926) a Catalan architect whose work is considered to be remarkable for its range of forms, textures and colours. His major works include the church of the Sagrada Familia and the Parque Güell in Barcelona.

Rodin: (1840–1917) a French sculptor, an impressionist in method and realist in execution. Famous sculptures include 'The Thinker' and 'Victor Hugo'. Although his work is now highly regarded it caused great controversy during his lifetime.

Léger: (1881–1955) a French painter whose work uses bright colour and contrasts curved and straight lines. His favourite subject matter included acrobats, cyclists and construction workers.

Elicit from students synonyms for *beautiful* such as *pretty, handsome, splendid, lovely, attractive, fair* and then encourage students to give reasons for beauty such as *elegance, symmetry, grandeur, colour, originality, excellence, pleasurableness.*

Do the students agree with the expression 'beauty is in the eye of the beholder' (idiom)?

2

1	creative	6	designs
2	artists	7	reputation
3	original	8	architect
4	masterpiece	9	restored
5	carved	10	potter

3

1	guide	6	gallery
2	curator	7	entry fee
3	exhibition	8	preserve
4	cases	9	alarm
5	display	10	reproductions

Reading: *Works of art* (page 170)

Description 1: a, b, f, i, j

Description 2: c, e, g, i, l, m

Description 3: d, h, k

Grammar: *indirect speech* (2) (Grammar Notes 16.1) (page 171)

A
1 Mrs Morse said that her daughter was getting married the next/following month.
2 Barry said that he went to the cinema every week.
3 Mr and Mrs Leech said/complained that they hadn't enjoyed their holiday at all.
4 Mr Barnes told me that he would make sure that the goods arrived in time.
5 The shopkeeper said that he couldn't order any more goods until he had sold what he had in stock.

B 1 'I saw a ghost last night,' claimed Sarah.
2 'I am going to stand for election to Parliament,' said Peter.
3 'I always take a packed lunch to work with me,' said Mr Blake.
4 'I will order the food for the party,' said Bernard.
5 'I have been waiting for you for half an hour,' said Lisa.
6 'Do you know what has happened to my cassette-player?' asked Jack.
7 'Where is the college on the map?' Mary asked me.
8 'Why didn't you take part in the race yesterday, Jenny?' asked Oliver.
9 'How do you manage to remember so many telephone numbers, Paul?' asked Lucy.
10 'What is the manager's name?' George asked the receptionist.

C 1 Tim accused John of stealing the camera.
2 Charles suggested visiting the exhibition.
3 Martin admitted setting fire to the house.
4 The Inspector denied meeting Professor Wilson in Zurich.
5 Norman apologised for being late.
6 John told Barbara not to skate on the ice.
7 Bill told everyone to wait for ten minutes.
8 Tom promised us he would do everything possible to help us.
9 Angela refused to make a statement to the police.
10 Christopher didn't know what to say/was lost for words/mumbled a few words.

Listening: *Visiting museums* (page 172)

Tapescript

MAN 1: I used to think I … I didn't like museums at all, in fact I … on the whole I don't, because a lot of museums are very badly organised …

WOMAN 1: Hmm … they're stuffy aren't they?

MAN 1: … they put things behind glass and in cases and you don't have much access to them but I went the other day to erm, the Museum of the Moving Image on the South Bank …

WOMAN 1: What's that? What …

MAN 1: Well it's, it's devoted to erm film, … it's a museum about film and television.

WOMAN 1: That's about the last 50 years, isn't it really?

MAN 1: (Yes … it goes back longer than that.)

MAN 2: (It goes back longer than that … yes …) it goes right back to the beginnings of, of …

MAN 1: … you know those Victorian erm … drums playing …

WOMAN 1: Oh yes, the erm lanternists of course, yes, that's right …

MAN 1: Yes, and erm you can see how moving images erm originated, and you have a … it's not … it's not stuffy at all, you have a chance to do things for yourself, like you have a chance to be a newsreader, you go into a little booth and you get cue lights and so on, and you can see yourself on television and all that sort of thing, the children absolutely adore it, and there's a wonderful er, compilation of clips from erm Hollywood musicals erm, it's it's I stood there the whole afternoon and watched it through again and again. It's brilliantly put together …

MAN 2: And they've got actors as well …

MAN 1: That's right, helping you through …

WOMAN 1: Showing you what's, what's, … Can you ask them questions?

MAN 1: Erm yes …

WOMAN 2: Yes, they're supposed to be in character. They're supposed to answer everything as they would …

MAN 1: (Yes, that's right they are …)

WOMAN 1: Like a Charlie Chaplin or something?

WOMAN 2: Nell Gwynn or …

MAN 1: Yes and they're sort of, pretending to be film directors and, … I mean it's all, it's all terribly exciting and children get ex … you know amazingly excited by it, but I remember being completely erm, really disappointed by museums when I was taken to them. I mean they get a terrible reputation among kids. I think and they … it puts people off for life …

MAN 2: Not the Science Museum because there again you can do things …

WOMAN 2: (Yes that's right) The only … we went recently to the Science Museum and my only criticism was the access for wheelchairs and pushchairs. It was appalling and you'd think that the Science Museum, a … you know, they'd have thought you know, technology has progressed so far that they'd have come up with something. I mean there was one large lift …

WOMAN 1: That's the worst thing about museums is the traipsing around, walking, walking, walking isn't it?

WOMAN 2: But they had some wonderful things, they had a Japanese robotics exhibition which was really entertaining …

MAN 2: (Oh, right …)

WOMAN 1: Which museum did you go to then, when you said … you started to say you hated it?

MAN 2: Oh no well … I mean just sort of the Natural History Museum, I remember being totally bored by …

MAN 1: I always remember taking my youngest son to the Natural History Museum …

WOMAN 2: (Hmm … Dinosaurs!)

MAN 1: … he was … he was about five and we saw all the dinosaurs and every time afterwards we drove by, he said, 'Oh look, the dead zoo!'

WOMAN 1: That's very good then!

MAN 2: But that's the whole thing about museums though is that most of the time you get the feeling that everything in them is dead and that one's going basically to a … to a … to a graveyard, do you know what I mean? and that's … I think that's what puts a lot of people off going to museums …

MAN 1: It's depressing …

WOMAN 2: And you have to pay as well …

MAN 2: Hmm … pay for the privilege …

A 1, 5, 7

B Good points: 1, 3, 5
Bad points: 1, 2, 4, 5, 7, 8

English in Use: *So, such (a)* (Grammar Notes **16.2**) (page 172)

1

1. The vase was so expensive the museum couldn't afford to buy it.
2. Patrick knows so much about Renaissance art that I daren't disagree with him.
3. The books are so old that they are beginning to fall to pieces.
4. He was such a famous artist that it was difficult for him to find time to paint.
5. It was such a heavy sculpture that a crane was needed to move it.
6. It was such a popular exhibition that people had to queue for three hours to get in.
7. It was such a long way to walk to the museum that I decided to take a taxi.
8. Anthony has read such a lot of books on art that he can answer all your questions.

2

1. There was such poor security in the museum that several paintings were stolen.
2. There was such severe damage to the painting that it could not be repaired.
3. It was such old furniture that no one was allowed to sit on it.
4. The expert gave such good advice that the museum always bought the right things at the right time.
5. They are such friendly people at the club that I always look forward to going there.

Reading: (page 173)

A Encourage students to mention ways in which museums could improve their services to the public such as *guide books in translation, more informative labelling of exhibits, controlling the crowds, providing refreshments, showing films and giving lectures, making sure they are accessible for people in wheelchairs or the blind.*

B 1 **Attracting children:** interactive exhibits, museum-trail worksheets, employing teachers, creating strong links with schools.

2 **Advantages of belonging to a museum society:** visiting museums for free or when they are closed, newsletter, social events.

3 **Two museums mentioned by name:** Jamestown in New England, Blists Hill Open Air Museum in England.

Reading: *Just as good as the original?* (page 174)

A The difference between a copy and a forgery depends very much on how the painting is signed, rather than on the skill with which it is painted.

Notes on the text

Samuel Palmer: (1805–81) an English landscape painter. His paintings have a mystical quality because he was influenced by the poet William Blake (1757–1827), whom he knew.

B

1	exact	7	picked up a bargain
2	traced	8	discreetly
3	set about	9	output
4	convinced	10	exposing
5	casual	11	cheated
6	took great delight	12	on account of

C
1 Keating faked more than 2,000 paintings.
2 Not all of his fake paintings have been identified.
3 As a young man, Keating produced copies for dealers.
4 Keating despised both art dealers and critics.
5 He didn't make himself rich by faking paintings.
6 Keating was ashamed of one fake Palmer which was not up to his usual standard.
7 Keating had a great sense of humour.
8 The charges against him were dropped on account of his ill-health.
9 He could fake a Samuel Palmer in about half an hour.
10 At the end of his life he received orders for his own work.

Talking Points (page 175)

Section 1

The photograph is of someone restoring a painting. Restoring paintings is a highly skilled job. The person needs to know a lot about the original painter, have a knowledge of the chemical effect of any products he or she uses, be meticulous and extremely patient.

Section 2

The photograph shows Andrew Lloyd Webber (composer of many popular musicals) who bought a Canaletto painting in April 1992 for 10 million pounds.

Listening: *Restoring works of art* (page 176)

Tapescript

Inevitably, works of art, whether they are paintings, sculptures, furniture, or buildings will deteriorate over time. Damage can be caused by damp or dryness, by light or by insects such as woodworm or moths. Sometimes very serious damage is caused by vandals. There are cases of people attacking sculptures with hammers, cutting famous paintings with knives or even firing guns at them. In the past, paintings were sometimes seriously damaged by people who were, in fact, attempting to restore them. Often, they used the wrong chemicals for cleaning and caused even more damage. It used to be common practice to wash paintings with soap, which does a lot of damage to the paint and owners of oil paintings used to rub them with onions to make them shine but the acid in the onion juice eroded the varnish.

If a work of art is not too badly damaged, experts will attempt to conserve it, that is they will make sure that no further damage takes place but if the work of art is in really poor condition it is necessary to restore it, that is, make it look the way it did when it was originally created. When works of art are extensively restored there is sometimes a lot of controversy about the result. The colours in a painting may seem very bright after it has been cleaned and to people who are used to the uncleaned painting the colours seem unnatural. Other people argue that those are the colours that the artist intended and that they are being seen for the first time for hundreds of years. If there is very serious damage, if part of a painting has been completely destroyed for example, the restorers have to make difficult decisions about whether to leave the painting in its damaged state and simply prevent further deterioration or to re-create the damaged part by adding new paint. This problem is particularly acute with buildings and statues which have been eroded by the weather. If the face of a statue is no longer clear, should it be left like that or should a new face be carved by a modern sculptor? Similar problems arise with the preservation of famous archeological sites. Should they be left as ruins or should they be partly rebuilt so that they seem more attractive to tourists?

A 1 Damp, dryness, light and insects such as woodworm and moths.
2 Attacking sculptures with a hammer, cutting paintings with a knife or shooting at them.
3 Washing oil paintings with soap, rubbing them with onions.
4 The colours seem unnaturally bright.
5 They have to decide whether to limit the damage or to re-create the original appearance of the sculpture.

Writing: *A report* (page 176)

A number of solutions are possible. Students must back up their arguments with evidence based on the information given.

English in Use (page 177)

1 I wish, if only (Grammar Notes **16.3**)

A 1 I wish/If only I hadn't bought it.
2 I wish/If only I had gone.
3 I wish/If only I had bought a ticket in advance.
4 I wish/If only I had taken a map.
5 I wish/If only I hadn't sold it.

B 1 She wishes she could tell the difference between a Rembrandt and a Rubens.
2 I wish I had (got) the catalogue.
3 I wish I wasn't/weren't working all day Sunday.
4 He wishes he didn't live in the centre of town.
5 I wish I could reach the shelf.

C 1 I wish/If only he would.
2 I wish/If only he would leave.
3 I wish/If only it would stop.
4 I wish/If only they would stop.
5 I wish/If only he would.

2 Phrasal verbs

1	win	5	date
2	paid	6	answered
3	sent	7	read
4	took	8	fought

3 Word-formation

1	qualifications	5	solution
2	pronunciation	6	permission
3	revision	7	inclusion
4	completion	8	repetition

unit 17 A SENSE OF ACHIEVEMENT

Lead-in (page 178)

1 The photographs show obvious achievements.

The top photograph is of a child sitting on top of his prize pumpkin which he has grown. The photograph below shows three ice-skaters holding up their medals and clutching bouquets of flowers.

Elicit vocabulary from students to do with success such as *feeling pleased/proud, effort rewarded, abilities stretched and tested, commitment, gaining recognition and acknowledgement, winning a medal, cheers of excitement, doing your best.*

2

1	under-achiever	6	effort
2	high-flier	7	concentration
3	precocious	8	setbacks
4	potential	9	entrepreneur
5	handicap	10	job

3

1	single-minded	3	pursue
2	boasts	4	struggle

5	victory	8	weather
6	commitment	9	risk
7	rewards	10	toll

Reading: *From scholar to entrepreneur* (page 180)

A Students should discuss the difficulties of interrupting your studies and the pressures on some young people to get out and start earning their living. How easy is it to return to education having already left?

B
1 withdrew him from school
2 provide the money to pay the debts
3 manage without
4 learn
5 succeeded
6 had intended to do from the beginning

C
1 False. Simon wanted to stay on and take exams so that he could go to university.
2 True.
3 False. He had borrowed heavily to keep the business going.
4 True.
5 False. He says he couldn't stand it any more.
6 False. They laughed at Simon when he asked to borrow money.
7 False. Most of them didn't take him seriously and only six joined him.
8 False. He says that the style of furniture turned out to be popular and they soon could hardly cope with demand.
9 True.
10 True.

Grammar: *gerund and infinitive* (Grammar Notes **17.1**) (page 181)

1 **A**

1	going	5	dealing
2	giving/making	6	going
3	answering	7	helping
4	being, stealing	8	applying

B

1	waiting	5	going
2	repairing/mending	6	being
3	working	7	helping
4	getting	8	having

2
1 to contact
2 to have witnessed
3 to be left
4 to have visited
5 to be living
6 to be accused
7 to have been killed
8 to be tested
9 to have been working
10 not to accept

3

1	wait	6	come
2	send	7	do
3	carry	8	go
4	dive/jump	9	keep
5	enter, win	10	pay

Listening: *A sense of satisfaction* (page 182)

Tapescript

KATE: Erm, I really don't like swimming very much and I'm not particularly good at it. I spend a lot of time hanging around the deep end fiddling with my goggles and my hat, er, debating whether or not I should dive in from this end or that end and watching all the other people and getting cold, and then eventually I pluck up courage to dive in and swim my twenty lengths which I find incredibly boring, erm, but everybody else seems to be doing it so you've kind of, got to, join in and erm, when I've showered and changed which is the bit I hate most, and recovered all my clothes and got my hair dry and er arrived home I just feel amazingly satisfied with myself! I can tell somebody I've been swimming!

DAVID: I like cooking which may sound strange. I actually like immersing myself in you know chopping the onions, the peeling, every bit of preparing a meal I enjoy and I also enjoy inviting people round and sharing a meal with them. There's a great satisfaction of having created a meal: three, four courses, cheese, drinks and so on and then having really good friends come round. Erm, I suppose there's some element of self-congratulation in it in that I could actually get it all together and organise it and have the food on the table for them but the real satisfaction is having people come round, have good food erm, a good evening and at the end of it the satisfaction of knowing they've had a wonderful time.

1
1 Goggles and hat.
2 She dives in.
3 'boring'.
4 Twenty lengths.
5 Changing out of her swimming clothes into her everyday clothes.
6 'amazingly satisfied'.

2 He mentions 1, 3, 5, 6.

English in Use: (Grammar Notes 17.2) (page 182)

1 **A**
1 general ability
2 general ability
3 specific action
4 specific action
5 general ability

B
1 could do
2 Were you able to find
3 was able to save
4 could see

2
1 manage to get
2 succeeded in reaching
3 succeeded in getting
4 managed to escape
5 manage to carry
6 succeeded in defeating
7 managed to finish
8 succeeded in making
9 managed to clear
10 manage to make

Reading: *A star is made* (page 183)

A These questions provide students with a chance to discuss their favourite stars and what makes some actors stars. Discuss things such as *good looks, outstanding acting, luck, good contacts, ambition* as ingredients for success.

Notes on the text

on the dotted line: a phrase used in reference to signing a contract

the hottest thing: exciting

Oscar: the annual film award presented in Hollywood

Golden Globe: an award presented by the American film industry

graduation: in American English, this refers to leaving High School; in Britain the word refers to leaving university after completing your studies

B 1 C 2 G 3 B 4 E 5 A 6 D 7 F

Reading: *Alonzo Clemons: Sculptor* (page 184)

A These questions allow students to discuss whether artists are born or made. They should talk about how artistic skills are developed, and also what status such skills have in particular cultures. They could also consider the relationship between artistic skill and intelligence.

B 1 A 2 C 3 C 4 B 5 B

Talking Points (page 185)

Section 1

The photograph shows the very close finish of a race. Students should discuss the feelings of both the winner and the person who came second. Is coming second better than coming in another non-winning position such as last? What feelings of achievement or defeat is the person coming second likely to have?

Section 2

This carries on the idea of winners and losers, with stories of people who have done something unusual, have failed in some way, or who have suffered or not been recognised as a result of their achievements.

Section 3

This provides students with an opportunity to talk about what gives them a sense of achievement.

Writing: *Applying for a job* (page 186)

In this letter students need to pay careful attention to how they present the details and to the tone they use.

Listening: *Writing a song* (page 186)

Tapescript

JAMES: Well for me there is nothing like the feeling of complete relaxation and total triumph after I've written a really good song, I feel like it's sort of a real release of a lot of sort of tensions and feelings. I sit down at my keyboard 'cause I've got a big keyboard I used to have a big old-fashioned piano but I've got rid of that now I've got a really swanky keyboard where I can produce lots of different sounds and string sounds and everything, and I get really excited sometimes. I come home and I sit down and I think … er … something's happened to me during the day and I've thought of a little tune or something and I sit down and I start playing about with that and then, and then, it expands and I think, 'Oh no, this is good, this is good, oh this sounds great, oh yes,' and then so many other things start to happen and then it's as if you get this huge rush of adrenalin and the time just flies by and you're not even looking at clocks or watches or anything and you're just sitting down there writing things, scribbling things down and then … you've finished, suddenly you've finished and you're playing it back to yourself and then, you know a whole night has gone by it's three o'clock in the morning and you've finished and you've created something complete and wonderful and you just think 'Umm! Umm!' and then you can just go to bed totally and utterly exhausted.

1 Relaxation, release of tensions and feelings, total triumph.
2 At a keyboard.
3 He can produce many different sounds.
4 Something that has happened during the day, or he may have thought of a tune.
5 He completely forgets everything else.
6 Utterly exhausted.

English in Use (page 186)

1

1	Wages	6	fees
2	salary	7	income
3	pay	8	interest
4	change	9	notes
5	cash, cheque	10	commission

2

1	took	11	how
2	that/which	12	moment
3	per	13	bit
4	about/with	14	been
5	main/chief	15	would
6	keen	16	school
7	team	17	can/could
8	in	18	question
9	says	19	all
10	who	20	like

3 **A** Phrasal verbs

1 let off
2 let … out of
3 letting … down
4 letting up
5 let … in

B

1 passed out
2 passed away
3 pass by
4 passed off
5 passed … on

4 Word-formation

1	illegible	6	illiterate
2	infrequent	7	inexpensive
3	irrelevant	8	illogical
4	incurable	9	insecure
5	irresponsible	10	irrational

unit 18 TIME AFTER TIME

Lead-in (page 188)

1 The picture shows a Dali painting entitled 'Melting Watches' and the photograph is a sundial at Jaipur, India.

Elicit from students vocabulary such as the months of the year and the different methods people use to be on time or have a sense of time such as *calendars, diaries, watches, clocks, alarm clocks.*

2

1 leap
2 working day
3 time zones
4 bank holiday
5 centenary
6 millennium
7 agenda
8 diary
9 calendar
10 clock

3

1 falls
2 orbit
3 jet lag
4 time span
5 pace
6 nostalgic
7 speculate
8 challenged
9 black hole
10 digits

Reading: *Give us back our eleven days!* (page 190)

A Note that only days, months and years have an astronomical basis, weeks do not. Therefore the easiest thing to change is the number of days in the week.

Notes on the text

Gregorian calendar: when the Gregorian calendar was introduced, religious belief was a matter of great controversy in Europe and since Henry VIII had broken with Rome in 1536 it was impossible for England, a Protestant country, to accept a calendar associated with the Pope in Rome

13-month year: one result of a 13-month year is that your birthday would always be on the same day of the week, as would festivals

B

1 orbit
2 fractions
3 made an attempt
4 mobs
5 yelling
6 appropriate to
7 adjustment
8 involve
9 proposals

C

1 The problem was that the dates did not correspond to the seasons. He solved this by having one very long year in order to get back to a reasonable starting point.
2 The purpose of leap years is to prevent the problem that Julius Caesar faced. The leap year uses up the 'spare' time and keeps the calendar in line with the seasons.
3 The leap years were every three years instead of every four.
4 The four-yearly leap year was introduced. (In the Gregorian calendar century years are not leap years unless they can be divided by 400 – hence 1900 was not a leap year.)
5 The Gregorian calendar was introduced.
6 Britain rejected it for religious reasons.
7 They were not well-educated enough to understand what was happening.
8 During the French Revolution, there was a desire to have a calendar which was rational, non-religious and represented a new start for society.
9 You might think that there were no advantages, but it was devised on a rational basis with names for months, with an equal number of days, that corresponded to the weather.

Grammar: *gerund and infinitive with or without to* (Grammar Notes **18.1**) (page 191)

1

1 signing
2 to sign
3 signing
4 seeing
5 to see
6 to see
7 to turn
8 turning
9 turning
10 informing
11 to inform
12 informing
13 to talk
14 talking
15 talking
16 taking
17 to take
18 taking

2

1 arriving
2 getting
3 paying
4 to buy
5 be
6 cycling
7 cycling
8 to ride

9	to buy	15	Being
10	getting	16	feel
11	cycling	17	to bring
12	going	18	mending
13	having	19	to bring
14	riding		

Listening: *Telling the time* (page 192)

Tapescript

In very early times, people could only measure time by counting days and observing the phases of the moon and the changes of the seasons. As early as 3,500 B.C. however, sundials were being used in Egypt and for thousands of years sundials were a popular way of telling the time. Some sundials were portable and were used like wrist watches, but others were enormous fixed structures, like the famous sundial in Jaipur, India which is 30 metres high. Sundials were not very accurate, of course, and neither were the water clocks that were used during the night.

Mechanical clocks were invented in Europe in the fourteenth century, although they are known to have existed in China earlier than this. These early clocks were operated by falling weights or springs and were very inaccurate. Although they could have hands and faces, they were usually designed to sound a bell at certain intervals. In medieval times people expected to hear a clock rather than look at one. In fact, the word 'clock' comes from the Latin word *clocca* which means 'bell'.

There was a significant improvement in the accuracy of clocks when, in 1657, a Dutch physicist, Christiaan Huygens, invented the first pendulum clock. He based his invention on ideas put forward by Galileo over 70 years earlier. Although pendulum clocks were quite accurate, they were useless on board ship. There was no reliable way of keeping time on ships and this was a major problem because longitude could only be calculated by using a clock that showed Greenwich Mean Time accurately. The theory of how to calculate longitude had been known since 1530 but there was no clock accurate enough to enable it to be put into practice. In 1714 the British government offered a prize of £20,000, an enormous sum of money in those days, to the first person to invent a clock that could be used to calculate longitude. John Harrison claimed the prize in 1735 but his first marine chronometer was not accurate enough. In 1760, however, his fourth chronometer satisfied the government's requirements. Even then, he only received half of the money and had to wait until 1773 for the rest.

Another big improvement in the accuracy of clocks took place in 1929 when the first quartz clock was invented. Quartz clocks are accurate to within one second in ten years and the majority of clocks and watches today use quartz crystals. In 1948 the first atomic clock was invented. This is based on the time it takes one atom of caesium to disintegrate and such clocks are accurate to within one second in 1.7 million years. Atomic clocks based on hydrogen atoms are even more accurate – one second in two million years – and scientists are trying to develop an atomic clock based on mercury atoms which would be accurate to within one second in ten billion years. Such clocks have great scientific value but they don't, of course have any domestic uses.

In 1987 two scientists designed a really amazing clock. It was a solar-powered clock that would orbit the earth seven times a day. It would have no face, but enormous hour, minute and second hands which would be visible in the sky. This clock would show Greenwich Mean Time, but a satellite clock in fixed orbit could show local time, so whenever you wanted to know the time, you could just look up into the sky. This space clock is, in a way, an extremely sophisticated sundial.

1	Egypt	15	one
2	3,500 B.C.	16	ten
3	30 metres high	17	1948
4	water	18	one
5	the 14th century	19	1.7 million
6	China	20	mercury
7	pendulum	21	one
8	1657	22	ten billion
9	1714	23	1987
10	£20,000	24	space/satellite/ solar-powered
11	to calculate longitude		
12	1760	25	orbit
13	reluctant/unwilling/ slow	26	seven
		27	sky
14	1929	28	sundial

English in Use (page 192)

1 Measurements

1 In nineteen thirty-nine the population of London was eight million six hundred and fifteen thousand and fifty.
2 The nearest star to the sun, Proxima Centauri, is twenty-four billion eight hundred thousand million miles away.
3 The room measures seven metres by nine metres.
4 He was born on the twenty-second of May nineteen-o-one.
5 A pint is nought (or zero) point five six eight litres.
6 One hundred and forty-four minus twelve equals one hundred and thirty-two.
7 Thirty-nine million six hundred and ten thousand five hundred and fifty passengers pass through Heathrow airport every year.
8 Three sixteenths, two fifths, two thirds, three quarters.
9 The temperature is minus ten degrees Centigrade.
10 This aeroplane can fly at three thousand five hundred kilometres per hour.
11 You are booked on flight BA five-o-one.
12 His phone number is o eight one, seven four o, double seven double nine.

2 Last, latest, least

1	last	8	last
2	latest	9	least
3	latest	10	latest
4	last	11	last
5	latest	12	last
6	last	13	least
7	last		

Reading: *Time travel* (page 193)

B 1 D 2 G 3 A 4 E 5 F 6 H 7 B

Reading: *The calendar calculators* (page 194)

A There are a number of ways of training the memory, which have been known since ancient times. They basically involve converting numbers and words into pictures because pictures are easy to remember. Similarly, there are various simple tricks that people can use to improve their mental arithmetic. Anyone can learn these, but what is astonishing about people like George and Charles is that they have worked these things out for themselves without being told about them.

Notes on the text

prime numbers: prime numbers can be divided only by themselves and one – 3, 5, 7 are prime numbers but 9 is not. Being able to work out a 20 digit prime number in your head is almost beyond belief

factor: the factors of 111 are 37, 37, 37

B

1	astounding	6	lagged behind
2	span	7	exquisite
3	with lightning rapidity	8	sniffed
4	swap	9	rocking/swaying
5	prematurely		

C 1 D
2 C
3 D

Talking Points (page 195)

Section 1

The two photographs show a modern kitchen and a medieval kitchen from Hampton Court. One obvious difference is the convenience of the modern kitchen (for modern-day times) but students might prefer the open fire as an oven or the size of the medieval kitchen.

Elicit from students the vocabulary of modern appliances such as *dishwasher, washing machine, microwave* and also other things such as *light, space, heating.*

Listening: *Samuel Pepys* (page 196)

Tapescript

INTERVIEWER: In the studio today we have Professor Bernard Wood, one of the leading experts on Samuel Pepys, the seventeenth-century diarist. (Hello.) Professor Wood, a lot of people have heard about Pepys's diary, even if they have never read it, but what about Pepys the man, do historians know much about him?

PROFESSOR WOOD: Well, yes, we know a lot about his life. He was born in London in 1633, the son of a tailor, and educated at St. Paul's School from 1646 to 1650 and then he went to Magdalene College, Cambridge from 1651 to 1654. Even when he was quite young, he was interested in political events and we know that he witnessed the execution of King Charles I in 1649. In the 1650s, as you know, England was a republic and Oliver Cromwell was Lord Protector. Pepys's first job was as secretary to one of Cromwell's supporters, Edward Mountague. He obtained this job in 1654 and a year later he married Elizabeth St. Michel, a fifteen-year old French girl.

INTERVIEWER: That seems very young.

PROFESSOR WOOD: Well, in the seventeenth-century it was quite normal to get married at that age. Of course, many people died at an early age. In fact, Elizabeth Pepys died when she was twenty-nine.

INTERVIEWER: When did he begin his diary?

PROFESSOR WOOD: In 1660. This was the year in which King Charles II was restored to the throne and Pepys, like many other people, had to reject the republican cause and declare their loyalty to the King. In this same year, he obtained an important position in the Navy Office, with a high salary and the opportunity to make more money by accepting bribes, which was quite normal at that time.

INTERVIEWER: What are the most important parts of his diary?

PROFESSOR WOOD: Well I think most people are impressed by his description of the Great Plague of London in 1665, when thousands of people died from a disease spread by rats, and his description of the Great Fire in 1666 when, although few people died, nine-tenths of London was destroyed. But for me the really interesting parts of the diary are his descriptions of everyday events, his visits to the theatre and to concerts and his comments on the people he knew.

INTERVIEWER: Did he keep his diary all his life?

PROFESSOR WOOD: No, no, he stopped in 1669 because he thought he was going blind. Actually, he didn't go blind but his eyesight became quite poor. You have to remember that Pepys wrote late at night by candlelight and he used a special form of shorthand which only he could read.

INTERVIEWER: Why did he do that?

PROFESSOR WOOD: Because he had many political enemies and there were comments in his diary that he did not want them to read. There were also things he didn't want his wife to read – she died in 1669, by the way, the same year in which he stopped writing the diary.

INTERVIEWER: Was Pepys a successful man?

PROFESSOR WOOD: Yes, he was. He became quite rich and in 1679 he was elected to Parliament but it was very important for him to be on the right side politically and towards the end of his life this became more and more difficult. In 1688, for example, he spent six weeks in prison in the Tower of London.

INTERVIEWER: Oh, why was that?

PROFESSOR WOOD: Because Pepys was a supporter of King James II, who in 1688 was forced into exile by Parliament. Once King James had gone, Pepys's career was at an end and he retired from public life in 1690. He spent the rest of his life building up his library which he left, together with his diary, to his old college in Cambridge. He died in 1703.

INTERVIEWER: Did people know about the diary at that time?

PROFESSOR WOOD: No, not at all. In fact, it wasn't published until 1825 and a complete edition didn't come out until 1983, so Pepys didn't really become famous until long after his death. He is certainly very famous now – a statue of him was erected in London in 1983.

1 educated at St. Paul's School
2 saw/witnessed execution of King Charles I
3 obtained first job (as secretary to Edward Mountague)
4 married Elizabeth St. Michel
5 began writing his diary
6 obtained important job in the Navy Office
7 Great Fire of London
8 Pepys stopped writing his diary
9 Elizabeth Pepys died
10 Pepys retired from public life
11 Pepys died
12 statue of Pepys erected in London/complete edition of diary published

Writing: *Telling a story* (page 196)

A This task is intended to revise and practise the use of the past simple, past continuous and past perfect.

English in Use (page 197)

1 For, during, while (Grammar Notes **18.2**)

1 during
2 for
3 during
4 for
5 During
6 While
7 while
8 During
9 while
10 during

2 Phrasal verbs

1 getaway
2 leftover
3 check-in
4 live-in
5 stand-by
6 knockdown
7 pick-up
8 follow-up
9 takeaway
10 walk-on
11 add-on
12 phone-in

3 Word-formation

1 weight
2 endangered
3 flatten
4 sticky
5 loosened
6 proof
7 reminder
8 bravery
9 passionate
10 shot

unit 19 EXPLORATION, ADVENTURE, INVENTION

Lead-in (page 198)

1 **A** Ask students to look at the picture of Isabella Bird (subject of the reading passage on page 198) a Victorian woman traveller.

An explorer is someone who travels to a country or region to discover something about it that has not previously been known.

A traveller is someone who enjoys travelling.

A tourist is someone who goes on holiday to a certain country or area for a few days or weeks.

B All of the pictures show means of transport which did not become popular. The first depicts a flying machine, the second shows a bus driven by steam.

2
1 supplies
2 hardships
3 exposure
4 endurance
5 transported
6 clung
7 assault
8 arduous
9 undaunted
10 ventured

3
1 error
2 original
3 patent
4 exploit
5 potential
6 version
7 device
8 technical
9 breakdown
10 superseded

Reading: *Inventions* (page 200)

A Students should discuss in pairs or small groups which inventions affect their lives most, which would be most difficult to do without and which give them the most pleasure.

Text 1 – E	Text 5 – H
Text 2 – D	Text 6 – G
Text 3 – C	Text 7 – A
Text 4 – F	Text 8 – B

B 1 the first form
2 changed in some way
3 invention
4 scope for development that would lead to financial gain
5 took out a special licence to stop others copying the invention
6 a boring activity that has to be done every day

C Encourage students to discuss their reactions to the inventions.

Grammar: *connectors* (page 201)

A 1 Ian didn't wear gloves despite the cold.
2 Jill had a bad cold but she decided to go ahead and make her speech.
3 They started a fire so that they could clear the land of trees.
4 While (I was) on holiday, I visited several museums and art galleries.
5 There is no signature on this cheque so the bank cannot give you money for it.
6 As soon as the gates were opened, the crowd rushed in.

B 1 whether … or not
2 in case
3 even if
4 not only … but also
5 as if

C There are many ways of completing the sentences. The following are examples only.

1 The soldiers waited until the enemy retreated before moving into the town.
2 You can have £50 in cash or a cheque.
3 They cannot be allowed into the stadium because they do not have tickets.
4 Jack put chains on his car wheels so that he could drive over the mountain pass.
5 He was allowed to begin his university course although he had not yet paid the fees.
6 You can collect your car as soon as it is ready.
7 Take gloves and a scarf with you in case it gets cold.
8 His novel did not win a prize even though it had been highly praised by the critics.
9 The police did not capture the escaped prisoner despite the fact that many members of the public claimed to have seen him.
10 He was not only the funniest comedian we had ever heard but also the most original.

Listening: *My favourite invention* (page 202)

Tapescript

INTERVIEWER: Which invention in your home is most important to you?

CLAIRE: Probably the piano because it's sort of an instrument I can relax to and it's something that only I in the household can do, erm, so it's my piano and I can just sit down and I can play for I mean, 5 minutes or sort of 50 minutes or an hour and it's just so relaxing I can just let all my emotions go and I can forget about everything else and it just produces such a nice sound as well. I mean because I'm quite musical anyway, just being able to listen to it and I think it's amazing the way you can just press a few keys and you get this magical sound out, erm, I don't know I think perhaps never having done exams on the piano has made me appreciate it more because I've always played music I've wanted to play on it, erm, one thing I do like doing is trying to improvise on it, I'm not so good at that but when I … when I'm in the frame of mind just sitting down and playing without any music, just improvising the music you want to hear and you made yourself is just a really nice feeling.

1 C 2 D 3 D 4 C

English in Use (page 202)

1	more	9	near
2	just	10	the
3	had	11	us
4	in	12	have
5	✓	13	✓
6	it	14	up
7	✓	15	✓
8	of		

Reading: *Clinging to life by the finger-tips* (page 203)

A Encourage the students to talk to each other in groups or pairs about everyday dangers such as *travelling in traffic, crime, air travel*, then get them to move on to more obviously dangerous activities, such as certain sports and exploration.

B

1	frail	8	agile
2	void	9	gradually
3	in his teens	10	addicted to
4	tougher	11	to its very limit
5	exponents	12	braved
6	assaulting	13	pursuit
7	lone	14	crucial

C 1 C 2 D 3 B 4 C 5 C

Reading: *The adventures of Isabella Bird* (page 204)

A Get the students to answer the questions in pairs or small groups and talk about the explorers and exploits they are aware of. Ask students to refer to famous explorers already mentioned in this course such as Raoul Amundsen; Christopher Columbus.

Difficulties explorers might have to meet are *lack of maps and knowledge of the area, dangerous or poisonous wildlife and plants, lack of transport.*

B 1 B 2 C 3 B 4 B 5 C 6 C 7 B

C
1. Her father was a clergyman.
2. She said she needed to travel for the sake of her health.
3. She wrote about her travels.
4. She started to plan major expeditions.
5. Her health improved.
6. Dr John Bishop.
7. It was conventional and she did not travel.
8. She looked like a frail woman but her travels showed her to be brave, strong and independent.
9. To the Atlas Mountains in Morocco.

Talking Points (page 205)

Section 1

The students should explore the topic of the pleasures and difficulties of living on a desert island, both alone and as part of a group.

The photograph shows a tropical island with palm trees, an idyllic beach with an aquamarine sea, a warm climate with plenty of rain and lush vegetation. There are no people and no animals.

Things people might need to live here are drinking water, food (whether naturally occurring or grown), shelter and warmth.

Encourage students to discuss how they would combat boredom and loneliness if there was no one else on the island.

Section 2

Students should cover the area of inventions, and follow on the discussion of Reading Passage 1 (page 200 students' book).

Listening: *Sewing machines* (page 206)

Tapescript

PRESENTER: In today's programme about inventions and the people responsible for them, we're going to look at sewing machines. Yes, sewing machines. Debbie Bolton has been doing a spot of investigating, and she's going to tell us all about them.

DEBBIE: Well, sewing machines have been around for about 150 years now, and it's quite interesting to look at exactly how they got invented. You know, often you can pinpoint precisely who the inventor was, you can point to one man – or woman – and say when and how they invented something. But with the sewing machine, there were actually a number of people who were very important in its development.

PRESENTER: So who's the best known person associated with sewing machines?

DEBBIE: I'd have to say that the person most people think of if you ask them that question would say, Singer, the American Isaac Singer. He's the person who set up a really successful company and ran a good marketing operation. But he wasn't really the inventor of the sewing machine.

PRESENTER: So who was then?

DEBBIE: If we go back to the very beginning, then we have to go back to the 1820s, and to a Frenchman called Thimonnier, Barthélemy Thimonnier. Towards the end of the 1820s, he made the first sewing machine. His business was quite prosperous for about twenty years, but the disturbances in 1848 caused it to fail.

PRESENTER: So did Singer draw on these ideas?

DEBBIE: No, he didn't actually. From Singer's point of view there were other developments that were much more influential. As I said, Singer lived in the United States and he got his ideas from what had been happening there. He was familiar with the machine that had been invented by a man called Elias Howe. Elias was an American too, and in 1844 he had tried to protect his invention by taking out a patent for the first sewing machine produced in England or the United States. Some of Elias's ideas in fact came from another man, called Walter Hunt.

PRESENTER: *Another man*. There seems to have been an awful lot of people with similar ideas.

DEBBIE: Yes, I told you that's one of the things that makes the invention of the sewing machine unusual. Let me tell you about Walter Hunt. He is most famous as the inventor of the safety pin, and in 1832, he built a machine that was an advance on Thimonnier's. Hunt's machine had a pointed needle and a double thread, which meant that the stitches were very strong, unlike Thimonnier's. His would have come apart if you had pulled them.

PRESENTER: Was Hunt's machine very successful?

DEBBIE: Well, actually Hunt wasn't really concerned about making money. He had a strong social conscience and he was worried that if his machine was successful, lots of workers would lose their jobs. So although he thought of going into business, he changed his mind and withdrew his machine.

PRESENTER: So this brings us back to Howe and Singer.

DEBBIE: Yes, that's right. Elias Howe was keen to see the success of his machine, and he sold it to a man in England, on the understanding that he would receive a sum of money for every machine sold. But unfortunately he was tricked, and got paid no money at all. Well he went back to the States after two years, with absolutely no money, and feeling very disillusioned.

PRESENTER: I'm not surprised. This doesn't sound fair at all. Were things any better for him in the States?

DEBBIE: Well, yes and no. When he got back, he found that his invention was becoming very popular and that other people, particularly Singer, were making machines similar to his. Singer's machines were technically more advanced, but Elias Howe felt that there were ideas copied from his machine. There was a court case, and as a result Singer had to pay Elias compensation. But it all worked out happily in the end. Elias Howe and Singer agreed to work together and produce the best machine they could. They both ended up as very, very rich men.

1 D 2 A 3 A 4 B 5 C 6 C 7 B 8 B 9 B 10 D

Writing: *Telling a story* (page 206)

Encourage students to write a good opening sentence. Make sure the story has a clear beginning, middle and end.

English in Use (page 207)

1

1	you	11	can
2	another	12	her
3	what/anything	13	enough
4	although	14	been
5	as	15	so
6	where	16	for
7	what	17	Like
8	than	18	talked/spoken
9	after	19	challenge
10	look	20	train

2 Word-formation

1	privacy	6	container
2	bleeding	7	conquest
3	slippery	8	sweeten
4	warmth	9	width
5	tendency	10	heating

3 **A** Phrasal verbs

1	Do up	3	do with
2	do without	4	do away with/do without

B

1	Hold on	4	held up
2	held up	5	hold on
3	held out	6	held down

unit 20 CONTRASTS

Lead-in (page 208)

1 The photo depicts The Natural Theatre Group, commonly known as 'The Eggheads'. The company is a street-theatre mime group which improvises comedy, basing their work on the mannerisms of their audiences. The people on the bench are laughing and smiling because the tourists look so funny and strange.

2

1	soft	6	fine
2	casual	7	experienced
3	mild	8	second-hand
4	simple	9	scheduled
5	natural	10	plain

3

1	E	6	I
2	J	7	C
3	F	8	D
4	G	9	B
5	A	10	H

Reading: *Grow up and get a set of vegetable dishes* (page 210)

A Ask students to work in pairs. If your students are still studying then ask them to imagine how they will change, whether they will retain the same ideas and ideals when they finish their studies and get a job.

B 1 C 2 G 3 E 4 A 5 F 6 B 7 D

Grammar: *adverbs* (Grammar Notes **20.1**) (page 211)

A **How?** quickly, badly, well, fast, easily
Where? at home, in the park
When? on Saturday, yesterday, at five o'clock
How Long? for two days, for six years

The order in the example is *manner, place, time.*

1. I met them on Saturday at the football match.
2. I saw Mary with her fiance in a restaurant yesterday.
3. The champion ran round the stadium slowly after his victory.
4. The burglar has to stay in prison for three years.
5. She was arrested for driving too fast on the motorway yesterday.

B These words answer the question *when*?

1. Our team rarely wins a match.
2. We will never get there on time.
3. I have rarely seen such interesting fossils.
4. He hardly ever arrives at 9 a.m.

5 The brushes should always be cleaned before being used again.
6 I can usually understand what she says.

C These words answer the question *how much*? or *to what extent*?

1 Samuel Castro was obviously an impostor.
2 David will definitely win the race.
3 He has obviously spent a lot of time in the sun.
4 They have undoubtedly committed these crimes together.
5 He might possibly have given the map to his brother.
6 She just removed the ring and walked away.

D 1 Jenny wasn't worried about the faulty lock – she just thought it was a nuisance.
2 Professor Jones wants to stop this project immediately.
3 I have received a letter from you this morning.
4 The pilot landed safely.
5 Helen desperately needed new clothes.
6 He easily forgot people's names.
7 I just wanted to let you know about it.
8 I am always the last person to know.

English in Use (page 212)

1 common errors

1 He gave me some advice about buying furniture.
2 Be careful not to lose your money.
3 Before going on holiday, we had the car serviced.
4 I suggest (that) you (should) ask for a refund.
5 Last year we couldn't visit New York.
6 He succeeded in winning the race.
7 They prevented the man from leaving.
8 He works as an accounts clerk.
9 His parents made him take the exam.
10 There is no point in waiting any longer.
11 It's a two-hour flight.
12 Society should not tolerate this kind of behaviour.
13 I like to remember the good times.
14 I sat in a comfortable, red chair.
15 People are very lucky to have a new hospital in their town.
16 It was such nice weather we had a picnic.
17 John watches television most of the time.
18 He is 25. *or* He is 25 years old.
19 At my college, you can play tennis.
20 Mr Brown is on holiday.

2 Else

1	someone	9	Where
2	anywhere	10	How
3	anything	11	Everybody
4	something	12	or
5	nothing	13	much
6	anyone	14	nobody
7	somewhere	15	or
8	What		

Reading and Listening (page 213)

A The tape gives one side of the story and the reading text a different viewpoint on the same event. It is possible to send half the class into another room to listen to the cassette, make notes and compare them with notes made by students who have read the text. The two groups can change round for the second story.

Tapescript

MRS ROBERTS: It was a shocking experience, I can tell you. I've never been so humiliated in all my life. We were on our way to visit friends and I decided to stop at the big department store near the roundabout to see if they had any children's pullovers – Thomas really needs some new ones. We pulled into the car park and to save time – we were in a bit of a hurry – I told Sam to stay in the car with the children while I just nipped into the store to have a look. I went straight to the counter where they sell pullovers and looked at them for a couple of minutes. I saw some I liked but I wasn't sure about the right size for Thomas. I was going to ask an assistant for advice but she was chatting with a colleague and just ignored me. I decided to just pop outside and try them on Thomas to see which size fitted, so I picked up two blue ones of different sizes. Obviously I intended to come back and pay for the one that fitted. I left the store and went back to my car. I was just putting one of the pullovers on Thomas when this man – I don't know who he was, he didn't say – just pulled the car door open, grabbed my arm and tried to pull me out of the car. I thought I was being attacked by a maniac. I was terrified, really terrified. I didn't want to get out. Then for some reason this man fell over. Then two other men and a woman arrived and just pulled me out of the car – they were really nasty. They spoke rudely to my husband and dragged me back to the store, calling me a thief and other nasty things. They locked me in a small room, just a cupboard really – it didn't have a window – for an hour until the police arrived. The whole thing is a disgrace, I'm completely innocent. I haven't done anything wrong at all.

B The differences between the two stories are:

Store detective	Mrs Roberts
spent five minutes looking	spent a couple of minutes looking
she ignored shop assistant	shop assistant ignored her
three green, same size	two blue pullovers, different sizes
identified himself	detective didn't say who he was
placed hand on Mrs Robert's shoulder	attempted to pull Mrs Roberts out
subjected to torrent of abuse	felt terrified
knocked over by car door	detective fell over
Mr Roberts threatened to use violence	detectives were rude to Mr Roberts
escorted to manager's office	dragged back to store
remained in manager's office	locked in cupboard
charged with theft	done nothing wrong

Other measures to establish the truth might be to ask other witnesses to come forward and to ask the store detective to produce the supposed 'stolen' items.

Tapescript

After we left the disco, we went to the club just round the corner. There were just two of us, me and my cousin Kevin. The bouncers on the door said that we couldn't come in because we weren't members but we know that you can join on the door but they wouldn't let us do that. They said that we weren't dressed properly but we were wearing smart but casual clothes. When we insisted on talking to the manager, two of the bouncers pushed Kevin over – he fell to the ground – and threatened to kick his head in. The other one grabbed my arm and twisted it behind my back. He then pushed me down the street. I felt a sharp pain in my arm which began to get worse – I was screaming but he still kept twisting my arm. After he'd gone, Kevin and I hailed a taxi and went to the hospital. My arm was X-rayed and it turned out that it was broken. It's in plaster now and the police are investigating the incident.

C

Doorman	Youth
four youths	only two of them
scruffy	dressed in smart but casual clothes
obviously drunk	not mentioned
stood in doorway	pushed Kevin over
youth became abusive	not mentioned
applied armlock	twisted arm
protested loudly	screamed
seemed all right	arm was broken and is now in plaster

Reading: *Mission Accomplished* (page 214)

1 Cassius is approximately over one hundred years old, as tall as a tree, has a tail, has a long tongue, has more than four limbs and swallows live animals.
2 The dinner is prepared by a domestic robot and Cassius eats the dinner by flicking his tongue and swallowing the animal in one gulp.
3 Because the chances of a major discovery were remote.
4 The ship will be destroyed.
5 At least 50 years.

6 He picked up a distress signal.
7 On water.
8 He was surprised by the freshness of the air.
9 They addressed him in his own language,using the terms of address appropriate to his rank.
10 Cassius has a number of choices – students can discuss this.

Talking Points (page 215)

Section 1

One photograph shows a little boy in a kitchen brandishing a toy gun; the other shows two girls in a bedroom playing with dolls and toys. These photographs suggest that male behaviour is active and aggressive while female behaviour is passive and quiet. Encourage students to put forward both stereotypical and non-conventional notions of male and female behaviour, both in children and in adults. Ask them if they think they conformed to the images in the photos when they were young.

Listening: *Town and country* (page 216)

Tapescript

MANDY: I was er brought up in the country but, of course, I now live in a town – a big town – the city of London and erm I'm really – (Clapham Junction?) Clapham Junction and I, I, you know, I like both. I can see why people like to live in the country, I can see why people like to live in the town but it's very difficult to, to if you carry on living in the country, this is how I see it now, to work, to find work. It's wonderful if you're bringing up children, I think it's ideal. But you're very cut off from people, you haven't got er you know roads full of people walking around at any given time of day which you have in London – erm you know your access is, is er prohibited.

KATE: Don't you find though that people living in the country are, er, rather narrow-minded in their views?

DAVID: I think that's a generalisation, (Mmm that's a generalisation). A lot of – quite a lot of great friends of mine live in the country, I wouldn't call them narrow-minded at all. I'd love to live in the country but erm – rather like you Mandy, I mean, it's just not practical. Er, so much of my work is in a town. Erm, I've sort of compromised 'cos I live slightly outside, erm it's a sort of half-way house, Richmond – and it does have open spaces and riverbanks and so on (Oh that's good.) which, erm well I mean I satisfy myself from that, from that point of view.

JAMES: I mean the ideal thing is to have two, two places (Yes exactly, I agree.) 'cos I absolutely *love* living in the centre of London. I think, I think there's just nothing to beat the sense of, er, excitement of being around where things are, are actually happening.

MANDY: Yes, I do I think it would, would be lovely to be in the city in the winter and er, and er, the country in the summer.

KATE: But you need to be rich to do that!

MANDY: Yes certainly and no ties!

DAVID: I, I used to think like you, I used to think living in the city was wonderful but I, I'm very disillusioned with big cities now and it's not just London, I think big cities have, they've degenerated, they're not er the big exciting places they once were and I don't think that's just me being that much older. (No.) 'Cos I used to feel very much like …

JAMES: But I don't know if I could handle living in the country for any length of time I think I'd go mad. I, I'd, I mean, don't, don't …

KATE: It does depend on whether you manage to establish a community or not.

DAVID: Yes. I mean you talked, I mean we were talking about, I mean you know, quality of life. But your life is obviously different. You have different values. What you want to get out of life is maybe …

KATE: Well, there's more variety in terms of things to do, (Oh indeed.) entertainment things, in the town.

DAVID: Yes but how often do you do it?

KATE: Well but you've got the choice. (You've got the choice.)

MANDY: Yes, when you have children it's difficult to get, get out to enjoy these things as much as when you're single.

KATE: But then do you need to be near them?

MANDY: But then all the children who live in the country that I know, when they come to London they absolutely love the recreation-grounds here in the city 'cos they're so wonderful. You know we've got nothing at home. So I think that's quite ironic really (Mmm, that's true.) They love coming to the city (Yes.) even though they you know, they live in fields surrounding their, their house and see cows every day.

A 1 difficult to find work
2 bringing up children
3 narrow-minded people
4 to live in the country
5 open spaces
6 the centre of London
7 two places to live
8 to be rich/have money
9 the same opinion as James
10 exciting places
11 go mad
12 quality of life
13 have children
14 recreation grounds
15 fields and cows

Writing: *Arguing a point of view* (page 216)

A 1 First and foremost
2 In addition
3 Furthermore
4 On the other hand
5 while
6 Besides
7 both positive and negative aspects

English in Use (page 217)

1 Phrasal verbs

A 1 g 6 h
2 d 7 j
3 b 8 c
4 i 9 f
5 e 10 a

B 1 c 6 j
2 a 7 i
3 e 8 b
4 g 9 h
5 d 10 f

2 Word-formation

1 robbery 6 sensitive
2 strength 7 spoilt
3 uncomfortable 8 boredom
4 relief 9 concentration
5 quarrelsome 10 successful

Exam Practice 4 (page 218)

1 1 efficiency 6 publicity
2 possibilities 7 weaknesses
3 illegally 8 security
4 excitement 9 inconvenient
5 activities 10 protection

2 1 B 9 D
2/3 A/C 10 B
4 C 11 D
5 C 12/13 A/D
6 C 14 A
7 B 15 D
8 A

3 1 I cannot carry more than/can carry no more than 50 kilograms.
2 The helicopter succeeded in rescuing all the ship's crew.
3 I apologise for not telling you about it earlier.

4 Steve had his watch stolen as he was getting on the train.
5 There have been many changes at this college in the last ten years.
6 My job is to give advice to the director on how to display the exhibits.
7 The director decided on the introduction of interactive displays for children.
8 Marina was full of admiration for the sculpture.
9 Jack's arrest came as a great shock to all his friends.
10 Sebastian made many appearances/ appeared many times on television.

4

1 ✓
2 do
3 it
4 ✓
5 here
6 ✓
7 ✓
8 being
9 into
10 ✓
11 others
12 those
13 try
14 to
15 heads

5 **Listening** (page 221)

Tapescript

Toffee is ten years old now and I've looked after him since my father bought him for me when he was three years old. We don't keep him in a stable, he lives out in a field all the year round. Horses need quite a lot of looking after. I suppose the most important thing is their feet. They can get things stuck there, things like stones, thorns, dirt and so on, so once a day I check Toffee's to make sure they are clean. Apart from his comfort, it's necessary to do this because there's a danger of infection, and of course if horses get an infection in their feet they go lame and then it's impossible to ride. And this would be a big blow to me because I love it so much. The next thing I have to think about is grooming. Because of where he lives, Toffee can get very dirty with all the mud and this is very unpleasant for him, so I use a coarse brush called a 'dandy brush' to knock all that off. But you mustn't overdo the grooming with a field-kept horse, because they need the oils in their coat to protect them against the weather. Water is essential, horses need a good supply of clean fresh water – stagnant water is very dangerous because it's got all sorts of bacteria in it. There's a big tank in Toffee's field and once a month, twice a month ideally, I have to scrub it out – not my favourite job, I must say. You probably know that horses' teeth keep growing all through their life – unlike humans – and they can have problems if the teeth grow sharp edges. So their teeth have to be filed quite regularly, every twelve months or so. One big expense is injections – horses need to be protected against tetanus and equine flu, and the vet comes and gives them these once a year. The final thing I should say is that in the winter, because it's so wet, Toffee wears a special rug to keep him warm and dry. It's not a good idea for horses to get cold and chilly.

1 field
2 feet
3 ride
4 mud
5 brush
6 coat
7 drink
8 once a year/every year/every twelve months
9 (equine) flu
10 (special) rug

6 **Listening** (page 221)

Tapescript

1 I saw this jacket in a shop and it had been reduced by about fifty per cent so I thought: that's really a bargain. So I tried it on and it fitted me and it looked good so I decided to buy it but just as I was about to pay for it I noticed a hole in one of the pockets. It was a very tiny hole, very easy to repair, but I pointed it out to the sales assistant and I asked them to reduce the price by £20 because, after all, it wasn't in perfect condition. They agreed and I felt very pleased with myself because it had already been reduced to half-price and now I had saved another £20. But when I wore it, I soon discovered that it wasn't as warm or as waterproof as I had expected and the pockets were very small and things kept falling out so it wasn't such a bargain after all.

2 I had ordered something from a mail-order company which sells very unusual and delicious sorts of food, mostly imported from other countries. In the catalogue, I had seen three boxes of various

types of food, one low-priced, one medium-priced and one high-priced. I ordered the medium-priced one but they delivered the high-priced one, so I just paid for what I had ordered, so they wrote and said I had to pay more but I said I have paid for what I have ordered. If you send me the wrong box, it's your problem not mine. You can either accept my money or come and take this box away and give me what I ordered. I was sure I was in the right legally and that they wouldn't take matters further. So in the end they just accepted my money and I kept the box, which I was pleased about because it was better quality, of course.

3 Well, I had been wearing these shoes for about six months when one day I noticed that the sole was coming away from the shoe and I thought, 'That shouldn't happen. They should last longer than six months. They were quite expensive.' So I took them back to the shop and complained. I didn't think I had a strong case because I had worn them a lot and they didn't look new but the manager of the shop apologised at great length, gave me a new pair of shoes completely free of charge and, in addition, a £20 voucher to spend at the shop next time I bought a pair of shoes. Well, I didn't expect that at all. I always buy shoes at that shop now.

4 I ordered a pair of trousers from a mail-order company but when they arrived I didn't like the colour because it was different from the colour in the picture in the catalogue. That's the trouble with ordering from catalogues – you are just choosing by looking at a picture not the real thing. Now this company offers to exchange anything you are not satisfied with so I posted the trousers back and asked for a different colour plus the cost of sending the parcel back. Well, they sent me another pair of trousers, which I liked very much, but nothing to cover the cost of sending the first pair back, so I was still out of pocket. I didn't take the matter further because the amount of money was quite small and writing letters and making phone calls would cost more money – but I still felt annoyed.

5 After six months it was obvious that something was wrong and they needed repairing or replacing but we weren't worried about this because the company which had sold them to us had given us a ten-year guarantee, so we were sure it wouldn't cost us anything extra. I phoned the company but I couldn't get through so I wrote a letter but it was returned by the Post Office who had been unable to deliver it. Eventually, I discovered the company had gone bankrupt. It just didn't exist anymore so our ten-year guarantee was completely worthless.

1 F 2 D 3 A 4 E 5 C

7 Listening (page 221)

Tapescript

INTERVIEWER: … so now the trip's nearly over, how do you feel about it?

STUDENT 1: Great.

STUDENT 2: Yeah, not bad.

INTERVIEWER: So tell me about the highlights of the trip. What have been the things that have really made an impact?

STUDENT 1: Well, there's been so many – but – yeah, the first day, in Paris, that was just amazing …

STUDENT 2: Yeah, driving in from the airport, early in the morning after the overnight flight, and then seeing the city – the river, and all those buildings I thought only existed on postcards …

STUDENT 1: … and then the shops!

STUDENT 2: No, actually London was better for that – there was more variety and it was cheaper …

STUDENT 1: Yes, you're right, but we were in London for three days and we had a chance to get to know it better, and to visit more. But I bought some great posters in Paris.

STUDENT 2: Yes, Paris was the best for art. We went to some marvellous museums. I bought lots of postcards of paintings.

INTERVIEWER: But you didn't just see two cities, did you? We're here in Dublin now …

STUDENT 2: This place gets my vote for street life. The city's got a real buzz. There's music everywhere. There are people playing in the streets, and then if you're thirsty and stop for a drink, you find there are groups performing there and you don't have to pay an extra penny to listen to them.

INTERVIEWER: What about the architecture? What do you think of the buildings you've seen here?

STUDENT 1: Yes, there are some lovely houses here, and the city is such a nice size. You can get around most places on foot. But the buildings don't compare with Athens. We saw a lot of temples there and they were so old!

STUDENT 2: But it was exhausting looking at them. There were so many tourists and the temperature! I was just boiling, we were all suffering in the heat. It's nice to have some cool weather here.

INTERVIEWER: I understand you've also been to Amsterdam ...

STUDENT 1: No, not yet. That's where we're going tonight. We have tomorrow there and then we're catching the night flight back home. We've been told all about the canals ...

STUDENT 2: And that it's expensive ...

INTERVIEWER: So how would you sum up the trip?

STUDENT 1: Great, but very tiring. Five cities in nine days is quite hard to take!

1 D 2 E 3 C 4 C 5 B 6 B 7 A